D1316918

MULTIPURPOSE
MAN

By the same author

The Broilerhouse Society

Friend of the Family

Patrick Goldring

MULTIPURPOSE
MAN

NEW YORK

TAPLINGER PUBLISHING CO., INC

First published in the United States in 1974 by
TAPLINGER PUBLISHING CO., INC.
New York, New York

Library of Congress Catalog Card Number: 73-18933

ISBN 0 8008 5424 1

Contents

Multipurpose Man

Erratum
An index was prepared but not inserted, and the
reference to it in the Table of Contents should be
disregarded.

For Polly, Hugh, Zachary and Sarah
approaching the world of work

Acknowledgements

For part of this book I have drawn on research done for *Drive*, the magazine of the Automobile Association. I am grateful to the editor, Mr William Halden, for permission to make use of this material.

My thanks are also due for kind help from the courteous and efficient reference staff of Richmond upon Thames Libraries, Mr Paul Mardon of the Industrial Society, Mrs J. Brown of the Amalgamated Union of Engineering Workers, Mr Ben Norris of the Musicians Union, Mr J. C. Hamilton of Nalgo, Mr R. J. Rodgers of Petfoods Ltd, Mr Ian Horsburgh and the very many correspondents in Britain and the USA who responded to an invitation to tell me about their experiences of double-jobbing. I am also most grateful to Miss Bridget Lunn for compiling the index.

Patrick Goldring

Chapter one

The mysterious rattle

Customers taking delivery of the gleaming products of the US car industry were puzzled by a mysterious rattle coming from some of the new cars. Nothing seemed to be wrong, yet the rattle persisted. Investigation eventually revealed screws left in brake drums or tool handles welded into fender compartments, defects deliberately built into the cars by assembly line workers who had chosen this way to express their frustration.[1] Other workers expressed their discontent by less mysterious forms of sabotage, scratching paint or slashing upholstery.

The mysterious rattle in the shiny car, the worrying sound indicating trouble in the expensive machinery, could stand for a discordant noise now being increasingly heard amid the purposeful roar of every advanced industrial economy. It is the sound of discontented and frustrated workers no longer willing to accept the boredom and stagnation of the conditions in which they have to earn their livings. Overt sabotage is still comparatively rare. But strikes in which the frustrations of boredom played a significant part have disrupted production in many industries, turning profit into catastrophic loss. In the car assembly plants, where boredom and fatigue are felt most severely, worried managements have noted rising absenteeism and high labour turnover.

Among the problems facing the advanced industrial nations in the Seventies, none is more difficult and dangerous or more widely neglected than boredom. If the problem is not solved, industrial unrest caused in part by the boredom of repetitive, unskilled, machine-paced work could become so widespread as to bring about economic disaster and a new age of Luddite machine-wreckers. Some of the more alert men in management are already looking beyond the era of strikes over money to the more difficult one of frustrations arising from work which offers no interest, skill or responsibility.

Mr Pat Lowry, industrial relations director of British Leyland,

Britain's biggest car manufacturers, sees the problem as one of education. He said in an interview:

> 'As the education system improves and produces better educated workers the problem will become more acute. With wider horizons they will take less readily to the discipline of the track. People today don't just hire hands. We hire the whole man, brain and all. For this reason we've got to look more clearly at activities of the brain as well. We want to involve the whole individual in the job, not just a pair of hands. We must create the right environment for a contented frame of mind.
>
> 'There's no doubt that the ostensible cause of a dispute, a wage issue, frequently conceals more fundamental causes —possibly the effects of discipline, the tedium of the track. People feel it and resent it, and we've got to find ways of eliminating or diminishing this resentment.'[2]

The theme was taken up by the Duke of Edinburgh when he addressed a conference in London organized by the Industrial Society. He told the assembled industrialists and trade union leaders:

> 'What is new and worrying is that modern industrial methods seem to have separated work from involvement. . . . I strongly suspect that . . . many people have come to the conclusion that money is not enough, that conditions of work are not all; material fringe benefits are insufficient compensation for uninteresting work. I suspect that much unrest is a symptom of frustration rather than greed. I believe that they would like the work to be more responsible and more demanding of their talents.'[3]

Repetitive, undemanding work has not just been invented in the past few years. Even the car assembly line has been with us for half a century. What has changed to make boredom an urgent and dangerous problem, as Mr Lowry noted, is the nature of the worker who has to do the boring jobs. Forty years ago, when unemployment was widespread, men were glad of any job and would endure any amount of boredom to keep it. Discipline was easily maintained by paying better-than-average wages for the soul-destroying assembly-line jobs. To feed their families men became part of the machine without complaining.

For most of the men who did the assembly line jobs a generation ago boredom was not the issue it is today. The assembly-line technique breaks down a complicated manufacturing operation into a series of small, simple operations. It was originally devised to make possible the employment of large numbers of barely literate farm-hands, with no mechanical skills, who could quickly and easily be trained to tighten nuts or carry out a thirty-second fitting process. The repetitive nature of the job was one of its attractions because it made available comparatively well-paid work to men who otherwise might have had difficulty finding any job and were not equipped for anything but unskilled labouring.

This approach to work still survives among the older generation. The middle-aged worker may hate his job but he usually stays in it if he can, knowing that jobs at car factory rates are not easily obtained by anyone over forty with minimum skills. This is true even in times of full employment: when the car trade is suffering a depression he is thankful to keep earning, however boring and exhausting the job.

Today's young worker is not restrained like his father by fear of unemployment and his own lack of education. Even when unemployment is high, losing a job is not the end of the world. The money may be good on the assembly line but he is not prepared to sell his soul for it. Nor is he prepared to tolerate an existence which in human terms is little more than a half-life: a dreary mechanical slavery during the day followed by an evening when he is too tired to do more than drink beer or watch television. The vision of himself doing this day after day, decade after decade, until he turns from a vigorous young man into a middle-aged zombie, fills him with revulsion.

The problem is most acute in the car industry because it is here that the work is dullest and the strains of assembly line work the greatest. Most of the skill has been taken out of the process of building a car and in its place there is only mind-dulling repetition, noise and fatigue. As one senior shop steward at Ford's Dagenham plant put it, 'Men here are slaves of automation. You'd treat a dog better than this, give it a longer lead than we're allowed. A man's work station is the length of the car body plus three feet each end and he has to stay in it. People using fixed tools can't even move that far.'

The assembly line worker must stay at his place on the track throughout the day with only a few breaks. To go to the lavatory he must wait until he can be temporarily replaced by a spare man. In the eight hours he is at the factory he is cut off from the outside world. As the workers see it, factory life is not far short of a term of imprisonment. Small wonder, then, that the more independent of the younger workers want to get out while they still have their health and strength. Nor is it surprising that the middle-aged worker, no longer able to break out but under increasing physical strain, feels resentment at the trap in which he finds himself.

If the assembly line worker has the most deep-seated cause for his discontents, there are similar rumblings in many other jobs today. The reasons are basically the same: workers are expected to spend their lives doing work which is well below their capacity and does not engage their minds. The money may be good, being employed at all may be something to which to cling in hard times; yet the worker resents his job as insulting to his intelligence, his skill, his capacity to learn and even to his manhood.

Unlike his parents and grandparents, today's worker is increasingly educated, alert, conscious of his personal dignity and aware of the possibilities the world holds. 'He watches television, he's been on foreign holidays. He knows there's much more to life than the factory can offer,' said one car firm's industrial relations manager. Others acknowledge that the worker educated beyond the requirements of the job is posing growing problems of discipline and discontent for the employer. What employers look for, said one personnel officer frankly, is the worker with a 'knitting mind' who can occupy himself cheerfully with his own thoughts while doing a routine job. Even when careful screening finds such men, however, the problem is not solved. 'The only thing that keeps me sane,' said one car worker, 'is thinking about my work as a shop steward. The operation I do is just up-down-bang, up-down-bang all day long. Most of the time I'm at it I'm thinking over plans for the next strike.'

The growing dissatisfaction of the intelligent worker in a boring job was acknowledged by *The Times* newspaper in a leader headed 'Why Are We All So Bloody-Minded?'[4]

'To less and less people,' *The Times* article stated, 'is it satisfactory to perform dully repetitive tasks with no intelligible say in what they produce or how they work. . . . There is at present a developing asymmetry between the kind of life and work to which an educated citizenry feel themselves entitled and the kind of work which a modern economy can offer even to the educated labour force it needs.'

The asymmetry is growing and the dissatisfaction is growing with it. It is already being expressed in horseplay, in careless work, in bad temper and touchiness which leads to quarrels on the shop floor and can boil up easily into an unofficial strike. Legal sanctions against strikers and their unions, it has been found, can do nothing whatever to curb this resentment. On the contrary, they have given industrial disputes an extra dimension of bloody-mindedness.

In various forms the malaise has spread far beyond the factory floor where it finds its most powerful expression. In many other areas of employment the same twin discontents are to be found: the middle-aged worker unhappily tied to the only job he knows, but one in which he is stale and unfulfilled; and the young worker unhappy at the prospect of spending his life making a living at a job which gives him no satisfaction, no challenge and no opportunity for the development of responsibility and additional skills.

Familiar figures in working life are the tired middle-aged teacher who finds children increasingly a strain and a torment instead of an opportunity, the salesman who no longer has the zest and energy to keep on top of the job, the shop assistant dreaming of wider horizons than the haberdashery counter, the secretary staying only long enough to accumulate savings to get away from office routine, the bus driver nursing an ulcer, the local government official stuck in a bureaucratic rut and snarling his frustration at the public, and the young, skilled carpenter who finds that his job exercises only a fraction of his skill.

Some of them are in jobs that would be dull for anybody. Some are in jobs which are dull and frustrating only to them as a result of their particular experiences and the way their particular personalities have developed. The feelings they share for a wide variety of reasons are those of boredom and frustration and a lack of zest for their work.

Inevitably the number of working people who share such feelings is increasing. Many factors in contemporary life contribute to the condition. Over a wide range of jobs less skill is needed as automation takes over from the skilled hand and the practised eye. For a few the new technology has brought more problems to solve; but for many more the solving of problems, the main interest of most jobs, has been totally eliminated. Not only on the shop floor but in the manager's office too, decisions which once required experience and knowledge of local conditions are now taken on the basis of the computer's print-out.

Increasing specialization and the breaking down of jobs into brief repetitive operations have led to loss of responsibility, variety and the interest of the unpredictable. The individual, with his dignity, his self-respect, his experience, his unique combination of qualities, is no longer esteemed and no longer needed. The skilled craftsman is a

13

fast-disappearing anachronism on the working scene. In his place are the assembly-line operator, the machine adjuster, the dial watcher and the quality inspector. Some have more responsibility than others but all are essentially servants of the machine, predictable, standard working parts of the industrial mechanism, easily trained and easily replaced when found to be defective, unreliable or worn out.

Quite apart from the job's intrinsic interest, or lack of it, frustration and discontent arise also from a feeling of imprisonment, of being owned by the firm. This was raised many times by workers at car factories in personal interviews. One said: 'There used to be a works tradition. We had a band, but it's gone now. So has the spirit.' A young worker remarked: 'I'm going to get out of here as soon as I can. I don't want to get stuck here all my life like some of the old men here have been. I'm not going to sell my soul to the company. My life comes first with me. I earn my pay; I don't feel I owe any special loyalty.' And another worker in his twenties: 'The Friday night shift can play hell with your social life. I skip it if I'm playing football on the Saturday.'

So strong is the feeling among young workers against being 'owned' by the firm that many employers who have traditionally provided good facilities for their employees are now reconsidering the form such paternalism shall take. Volkswagen, the German car giant, have given millions of marks to provide houses, churches, schools and public buildings at Wolfsburg and to establish company holiday resorts. Yet the company policy is against providing social clubs for the workers. The firm says: 'We want nothing to do with their leisure activities. That would be trying to stamp VW on their foreheads.'[5]

More often than not, the firm is there to be fought for higher wages. Rightly or wrongly, it is often the butt of resentments which arise from the strain under which the man works and from his sense of wasting his life. The more boring, tiring and unfulfilling the job, the more determined is the worker to preserve his personal independence.

Probably the most important of all factors making for discontent and frustration at work are the spread of education and the widening of horizons. Whatever criticisms may be made of the quality of modern education, there is no doubt that many youngsters leaving school today have a sense of their own personal worth. They feel that they have a right not only to earn a living but to do so in a way which engages their talents and their interest. And they feel a keen resentment if this expectation is not satisfied.

Their education has taught them more about the possibilities of life than their fathers or grandfathers knew. Television, cheap holiday travel and the ability to move about by car have opened up the world to them in a way that often makes it seem to them intolerable that they should be shut in a factory, office or shop all their working lives. Most young workers are, and feel themselves to be, capable of much more than unthinking routine. They feel they have a contribution to make to society and resentment rises fast if they are not asked to make that contribution.

It is true that one of the effects of the school system may sometimes be to make the youngster who has done badly in it feel a failure. But if it does, this is not the making of a loyal and contented worker. If the education system labels him a failure he may still catch the independent spirit of the age and feel, not that he is an educational failure, but that the education system has failed him. In this he will be right; and far from making him more cooperative, it is likely to increase his resentment.

Personnel officers seeking men for repetitive, dead-end jobs still look hopefully for the less intelligent school-leavers and young men, in the belief that these will settle more happily and tractably to the discipline of the assembly line. But in the lower age brackets those who are prepared to give their lives unthinkingly and undemandingly to whatever task they are put to are a rapidly diminishing band.

Young men and women today are not fools. They have been around. They know the score. They are acutely conscious, many of them, that they have only one life to live; that there is more to life than take-home pay; that life could be exciting, interesting and rewarding in ways other than financial. They have a lot to give and it is more than many employers are equipped to take. A new, educated, intelligent work force is being created at a time when many jobs are being drained of whatever content of skill, responsibility, variety and problem-solving they once had.

This is a formula for discontent which not even the growth of unemployment can damp down. Far from rising unemployment having the disciplining effect that some employers hoped for, it has added to the restlessness and dissatisfaction of people who are still at work. In many boring and fatiguing jobs security and comparatively high earnings are the only attraction. If the growth of long-term unemployment takes away the security, and seasonal lay-offs and

15

short time reduce the average earnings, such jobs have nothing to recommend them and resentment at being tied to them rises accordingly.

To these frustrations and resentments have been ascribed much of the industrial unrest which has beset the advanced countries in recent years. Absenteeism, careless and even deliberately bad work, falling productivity and a tendency to strike for no sufficient reason have all been seen as results of the growing revolt of the bored. One writer on the theme of frustration as a cause of inflation has this to say:

> 'There is a known tendency for people who are frustrated to become unduly aggressive and irrational. Equally dangerous, they are far more likely to display an exaggerated sense of solidarity with their mates. "My union right or wrong" is a natural reaction of frustrated people bound together by common grievances and a common material interest.'[6]

From this he argued that 'a few groups of frustrated, trigger-happy workers can generate inflationary pressures throughout the economy'.

In the face of this problem and the economic ills it threatens, several solutions have been put forward and tried out with varying degrees of success. One of the earliest responses, still to be heard from some industrialists, was that the boring nature of work was one of the facts of life that workers had to put up with and for which they were amply compensated by paying them skilled rates for unskilled work. What more could they possibly want, except piped music, which unfortunately could not be supplied because of the high level of machinery noise? Along with this goes the thought that workers like boring, repetitive jobs because it gives them time to think about something else. Women workers in particular are cited as liking mindless work because they can gossip or, if the noise does not permit that, dream about romantic adventures, A leading industrialist has cited the popularity of fishing as showing that what might seem boring was really soothing and relaxing. Workers only thought they were bored, he said, because outsiders like industrial psychologists and journalists told them that they were. If everybody minded his own business, men on the assembly line would be quite content.

More rational, with a pedigree going back to Marx, is the proposition that the worker will enjoy his job more, and fulfil himself as a person, if he knows what his work is for, if he understands, approves and participates in the social objective to which it contributes. There is a good deal of truth in this. In time of war, munition workers and men assembling tanks can be inspired if they are shown the vital significance of their work in the total strategy, or introduced to the heroes who use their munitions or drive their tanks. Always provided, of course, that the war in question is one which the workers concerned support: a visit by a US Air Force veteran of Vietnam to give a pep-talk at a napalm factory might have other effects. In peace-time, when social objectives tend to be less compelling, a boring job may not be much less boring when the worker fully understands that the company's profit and the shareholders' dividends depend upon his doing his part conscientiously and accurately.

Much was hoped from this sort of motivation in Russia, where production is for social use instead of private gain. But even there it seems clear that in spite of constant exhortation and propaganda the boringness of a boring job has not been eliminated as successfully as was hoped. The truth seems to be that this understanding is a positive and useful factor when combined with others but is not an answer on its own.

For repetitive industrial jobs the most hopeful form of amelioration today is the concept of job enlargement or enrichment. In most factory jobs this is interpreted as enlarging the worker's task from one small operation to a series of operations which amount to a sizable transformation of the product. Thus a worker who would be bored into a stupor soldering two wires into a radio set as it moves past on an assembly line would feel the interest of a personal challenge and achievement if allowed to assemble the whole set. The concept also calls for workers to be given more control over their working conditions, in particular to set their own individual pace and to work in their own ways, and to be given more responsibility for checking quality and finish. In job enrichment programmes the workers are treated as far as possible as intelligent and responsible human beings.

Where such concepts have been applied the result has usually been a remarkable improvement both in employee morale and in profit. But what is most remarkable about job enrichment schemes is the revelation they provide of the inefficiency as well as the inhumanity of those allegedly scientific production methods which take little or no account of the thoughts, feeling, aspirations and self-respect of employees. When job enrichment was introduced at the Corning

17

glass works in Medfield, Massachusetts, meters formerly produced on an assembly line were assembled individually. After the change, inspections were reduced, the proportion of rejects dropped and profits went up. Assembling the whole meter gave each worker a feeling of personal responsibility, pride and interest in the job, with beneficial effects on quality, reliability and speed of output.

A similar approach, giving employees more discretion in the way they do their work and in devising new work methods, has had equally heartening results at Imperial Chemical Industries in Gloucester. 'Helping people to work together rather than in solitary competition and to work together at more rewarding jobs—these are objectives that will attract idealistic younger workers', a writer in *Fortune* noted.[7] Other enthusiasts in the same cause have been delighted to find that laundry employees work better in small teams with their names on the newly-laundered shirts returned to the customers.

After years of being treated as a crank notion, it is now conventional wisdom among enlightened managements that people who are treated as thinking human beings are more likely to work better and more intelligently than people who are treated as zombies. It has been a long, hard struggle but this particular message has now made something of a break-through in parts of industry.

Important though this is as a concept in improving employee relations, however, it is not by any means a complete or universally applicable answer to the problem of the boring, psychologically unrewarding job. In the first place, its application is most limited in just the situations which need it most. A meter factory run on old-style assembly line principles, for instance, will undoubtedly be a boring and oppressive place in which to spend a working life, but not nearly so mind-deadening and inhumanly regimented as a car assembly line can be. A meter may be taken from the assembly line and assembled from start to finish by one person at his own pace, without loss of profitability. Cars, on the other hand, cannot be built one at a time by one man or a small team without an escalation of costs which would make the operation wholly uneconomic in the family car market. The car worker's job can be enlarged if he is given a sequence of operations to perform, and this is done in the Volkswagen factory and elsewhere. This makes the job more acceptable by introducing some variety and movement—the worker follows the car some way along the assembly line before going back to start the process again. And if the sequence of operations is long enough for the

18

worker to see the sizable difference his contribution has made to the building of the vehicle, some psychological satisfaction is gained. But whether he does one thirty-second operation over and over again or a series of operations lasting several minutes and involving a short walk down the line, he is still doing a repetitive, unskilled job which is probably far below his capacity. While variety and movement may be added to the job to make it more bearable, it is still in essence the same job.

The same holds true for most of the jobs to which the panaceas of enlargement and enrichment may be applied. It would be wrong to underestimate the very real gain in social acceptability which results from humanizing the conditions under which the job is done. Undoubtedly a happier working atmosphere can be created by treating working people as people and not just as workers; this is a very real benefit to the work force and management alike. But it is not the whole story or even the main part of the story. Conditions may have been improved, but an unskilled job which has no real problems to solve and does not need the skill or knowledge that could be applied in other contexts, remains the essentially boring and unfulfilling task it always was. In a sense, the worker is being deceived by a conspiracy to pretend that two dozen unskilled operations performed in sequence amount to a skilled job. The deception is a benevolent one but it glosses over the fact that a difficult problem has not really been solved.

Even where job enlargement has been applied and inhuman conditions have been humanized as far as possible, a number of problems remain to be solved if the revolt of the bored and frustrated is to be turned from destructive to constructive ends. There is the problem of variety, the fundamental human need for a change of scene and subject which rests and refreshes the mind and wards off depression. There is the human need for people to feel that their lives have meaning and importance. There is the need for fresh challenges to face, the need to feel that life still has new experiences to offer, the need to feel able to improve one's skill and knowledge and better one's prospects, the need to be able to gain the confidence and respect of other people.

Perhaps above all, there is the need to feel free. The man or woman who is tied to a job, even a good job, may feel frustrated and confined. Man was not meant to be a caged animal, a piece of machinery, a domestic beast, a galley-slave or a company man. It is not enough to provide him with a comfortable and well-aired cage and point to its superiority over his old and smelly one. Education has raised his sights; nothing less than genuine freedom will do. How is this to be attained?

Chapter two

A change is as good as a rest

In a working situation the bored, the frustrated, the exhausted, the stale, the discontented and the disappointed share at least one source of unhappiness: they are all in need of a change. Many of them need change in the most immediate and literal sense. They are bored with their jobs, they feel shut in and imprisoned, they are working at jobs that give them no satisfaction, or they have ambitions to work at something else. Others need change more as a possible option; they would like to feel that they could switch jobs if they wished. Given a clear, practical possibility of change, the assurance of freedom for the taking, they might well feel less discontented with their present employment.

The feeling that one could be doing something else, that one is not irrevocably tied down for life, can be an important factor in personal contentment. It is right that it should be. We live in a society in which the concept of personal freedom is highly regarded. We regard political freedom as essential if life is to be tolerable. We pay lip-service to economic freedom. But for most people freedom to organize an individual way of working and to change jobs at will is illusory. At a time of high unemployment they are thankful enough to have a job at all. Even in good times when work is plentiful, changing jobs is no easy matter. Inertia, seniority, experience and, very often, pension arrangements tie the worker to one employer until retirement, dismissal or the collapse of the firm. To change jobs would mean acquiring a new skill, starting again at the bottom and almost certainly a drop in earnings substantial enough to deter a worker with family commitments.

The problems posed by the revolt of the bored can only be met by large-scale change in the whole working situation. Not only must change be made a realistic option in the worker's life. There must be a change in the way society looks at work. It is time for the emergence of Multipurpose Man.

Multipurpose Man is the worker with more than one skill, more than one working interest, more than one job. His outlook and his approach to work are quite different from those which have been usual until now. He sees no special virtue in the cobbler who sticks to his last. The jibe about a jack of all trades being master of none he rejects as a piece of reactionary brain-washing designed to keep him in his place. The worker with this new outlook believes that man is a many-sided, adaptable, questing and ingenious creature whom nature never intended to be shackled to one small and often insignificant task all his working life. He sees no merit in giving a lifetime's loyalty to one employer or to one employment, or in spending all the week at one job. He does not reject the concept of one full-time job if the job itself is sufficiently stimulating in its variety and challenge. But he is concerned to create a working life for himself which must be challenging and fulfilling to him as a man as well as materially rewarding.

To achieve the variety and interest he needs in his working life, he will wish to create his own pattern of work, spending perhaps half the week on one job and half at a completely different one. He may want to change not only jobs but industries every few years. He may split the working week, or the working month, among three or four employers, avoiding a lifetime commitment to any one trade or occupation. He will experiment, seek fresh work horizons, find out the employments that best suit his talents and his temperament, and mix his own particular work cocktail to suit his own individual taste.

To Multipurpose Man the closed, repetitive world of the assembly line factory will never be the prison of discontent it can become for the man who spends his whole working life in it. For a morning or an afternoon, or for two or three days a week, assembly-line work can be almost a relaxation, offering valuable, well-paid time while the mind lies fallow between spells of more creative work. For half a week exhaustion and strain do not become a problem. There is no depressing and frustrating prospect of the same work being continued until retirement; the hostilities that assembly-line workers now increasingly feel need not arise. With a limited commitment, time-keeping and absenteeism need no longer be troublesome. The simple process of cutting the job in half could make it not only more tolerable but actually agreeable.

For the rest of the week Multipurpose Man would seek another half-time job which would provide whatever ingredient was most important to him individually. One man might do an office job because he valued the status. Another might become a probation officer

22

because the social service element particularly appealed to him. A third might complete his week by cab-driving, a fourth by working as a gardener, a fifth by serving in a shop. Some men might go all out for money and try to get two jobs with high pay. Others would value movement, interest, meeting people or working in the open air and seek half-time jobs accordingly.

The advantages of such a two-job economy would not be confined to men and women doing dull jobs. Even in some highly skilled occupations it is difficult to maintain top form all the time. Indeed, the more demanding the job the more likely it is that the man doing it will become stale at times and give less than his best. A salesman cannot be at his most persuasive every moment of the working week. If he worked at selling for only half the week his effectiveness would probably rise during that time, particularly if he combined the job with another in which his persuasive powers were not called upon. Teachers, surgeons, administrators can all fall below their top form through staleness. Many would be all the better at their chosen profession for working shorter hours at it.

In many jobs the moving and mixing would themselves improve a man's all-round ability. A repetitive worker would gain fresh alertness from change. A teacher would gain knowledge of the world, to the benefit of his pupils, by spending half the week in business. Multipurpose Man has, in fact, already established himself in the teaching world. Many art teachers spend two or three days a week teaching, thereby earning enough to support themselves while they paint. Their pupils gain from being taught by a practising artist; the teachers can devote themselves to art without worrying whether a painting will pay the rent. The coming of Multipurpose Man would spread similar benefits among other workers.

The concept of the two-job man put forward here differs radically from the concept of the moonlighter or the part-timer as we know him—or her—today. It entails the adoption of a completely new attitude on the part of workers, employers and society at large towards the nature and purpose of work. It is not just a matter of timetabling. It requires the abandonment of many long-cherished prejudices and a change in the climate of society.

It requires first of all a change in the popular attitude to work and leisure. For all but a few in the professions, the arts and the dwindling crafts, work is not an experience to be enjoyed for its own sake, but a necessary ordeal which brings the benefits of a living wage and, if the worker is lucky, a chance to exercise a skill and an opportunity

23

to form a social relationship with a group of congenial fellow workers. Whatever the worker is really interested in has to be cultivated in whatever time he has available outside working hours.

This can lead to some strange effects. It means that a worker will often spend exhausting hours after a hard day's work doing the things that give him the interest he does not get during the working day. He may spend several nights a week on social work which gives him the responsibility and human contact he misses in his paid occupation. He may spend all his spare time on do-it-yourself jobs about the house, on gardening or on a hobby, because these enable him to satisfy a creative urge which finds no outlet during working hours.

The worker's day is divided sharply into work, from which little real satisfaction may be expected, and leisure, in which all the activities which engage his interest as a human being compete for the fagend of his day. Whatever he does in this latter limited period involves denying himself some other sphere of activity. If he gives himself up to social work he has little time for sport or gardening, though he may need these recreations more than his neighbour who makes no such voluntary contribution. If he devotes himself passionately to a hobby he may have to give up most of his social life. If his paid job is a physically hard one he may have no energy left for recreation, though he may need it more than most of those who have the time and energy for it.

There is the further paradox that the man with a job may have too little spare time to develop all his interests and enjoy some recreation; while those without jobs, having plenty of time to spare, cannot pursue their interests for lack of money. It will clearly be necessary to break down the barriers between work and leisure, to put more interest and personal fulfilment into work, to provide payment for much of today's voluntary work and to regard all activity as part of life and potentially contributing to the interest of living.

Part-time work and moonlighting at present enjoy low status because they are largely restricted to unskilled jobs and low-status workers. There are some notable exceptions, as we shall see, but the present profile of the British or American moonlighter is a man in a relatively low-paid full-time job who works part-time at another job solely to increase his earnings and often to the detriment of his health. A probably inflated recent estimate is that four million British workers have additional jobs[1] and a similar figure has been calculated for the USA. Typical examples are teachers working as insurance salesmen, firemen and policemen as painters and decorators, clerical workers as TV repair men and plumbers as dance-band musicians. Professional employees such as accountants and lawyers tend to stay within their professional field; a big company's accountant, for instance, working in the evening for small businesses.

The typical American moonlighter has been described as a comparatively young married man with children who feels a financial squeeze.[2] He has a full-time primary job and works thirteen hours at a different line of work. Teachers, policemen, firemen, postal workers and farmers are among those most likely to have second jobs. Many work for themselves part-time, run farms or businesses or are sales and service workers.

Two groups of moonlighters who enjoy higher status because of their skills and because their moonlighting is not solely to make up for a low-paid main job are people in the educational and communications field and part-time musicians. The professor who makes frequent appearances as a TV pundit is extending the scope of his main job and possibly (though also possibly not) enhancing his professional reputation. He is not usually thought of as a moonlighter, though he fits the definition of one. The part-time musician is also a special case. Though the money is useful he is often seen, and sees himself, as someone who is lucky enough to make his leisure activity pay.

Part-timers whose part-time jobs are their only means of livelihood also rate poorly in public esteem. This, too, derives from the low pay and lack of skill usually associated with part-time work. Many part-timers are housewives with young children who cannot spare time for a full-time job but go out to work for a few hours a day to augment the family income and gain a little social interest. In the past they have tended to earn lower rates than full-time workers, but pressure from trade unions has brought their rates in line with those of full-timers doing the same job. However, the job itself, typically repetitive assembly or packing work in a factory, tends to be unskilled and its status consequently low.

From the fact that part-time working rates low in public esteem, it is tempting to equate part-time work with unskilled work and to assume that any really serious job must be worked at full time. There is no necessary reason why this should be so. Society despises part-time work because part-timers are usually poorer, less skilled and less educated than the average. This is in spite of a finding by the US Bureau of Labour Statistics that the average moonlighter is hard-working, ambitious and determined to raise his status.[3] The same survey noted also that two frequently found forms of moonlighting and part-time working fall outside the usual pattern of the ill-paid trying to augment their income. One group, the largest group of double-jobbers in the USA, were basically small farmers who worked in factories to pay their way while they built up their farms. The other groups were men without capital who worked in their spare time to build their own businesses to the point where they could leave their employment. Their main motivation was to be their own bosses.

If more highly paid, highly skilled and highly educated people did part-time jobs, part-time working could enjoy prestige equal to full-time work, and the jobs available to part-timers would include the 'serious' sort now reserved for full-timers.

This raises the question of the status of work itself. At present, certified skill (evidenced by a diploma or an apprenticeship), long experience (evidenced by having been around a long time), and dedication (evidenced by willingness to work night and day at the job) are all esteemed virtues and enjoy high regard. There is correspondingly low regard for any work in which one can become adept after a relatively short training period and in which a half-timer can make a significant contribution. In jobs of this kind the low status accorded to part-timers is accorded also, though to not quite the same extent, to full-timers. If they work in a job that part-timers can do, the feeling is, it cannot be really serious work.

Traditionally craft trade unions have protected the status and exclusive nature of their skills even when their members have not needed to employ them. One of the problems besetting the car industry is that many workers have higher skills than their jobs need. What these skilled men actually do in the car factory, very often, could be done by any reasonably intelligent worker with a little training. If they stay in car factories for long periods, skilled men often lose their full skills for lack of practice. Yet they need to maintain them because their skills will be required if their car factory employment ends and they have to seek work as tradesmen elsewhere.

Just as traditional skills can in some circumstances be overrated commodities, so also the value of long experience is sometimes exaggerated. Six years' experience may be better than six months' experience; but there comes a time in many jobs when added years of experience bring only increasing resistance to new thinking. A worker may need experience to know the full dimensions of a job; but the longer he spends in one job the narrower his outlook becomes. After a time length of service in itself becomes an asset of steadily decreasing value. Ripeness of judgment is often cited as one of the fruits of long experience. But the judgment is likely to be more mature if the experience has been wide and varied. It is often said of a man who has been doing the same job all his life that he knows it so well he could do it in his sleep. The danger is that if he has been doing it too long he probably *is* doing it virtually in his sleep. Long experience is most useful when it can be tested and applied in new situations.

Dedication, in the sense of a willingness to work excessive hours, is another quality hitherto given unqualified approval which deserves to be looked at with some scepticism. If a man consistently has to take work home or spend long hours on regular unpaid overtime there is something wrong with the man or the job, or both. If he does a great deal of regular paid overtime this may simply be because the present prejudice against part-time work prevents the rational organization of the work into two part-time jobs. In any event there is no special virtue in the sort of dedication which leads to consistent overwork. The man who does this may be dedicated, but he is also probably tired, neurotic, narrow in outlook, stale in his thinking and unhealthily obsessed with his own indispensability.

It is not suggested that skill, experience and dedication are all worthless concepts; only that they should not always be accepted at face value without any attempt to ask what they really contribute to a particular job. We should not write a man off as a dilettante, insufficiently serious about work to do a proper job, if he wants to devote only twenty hours a week to it instead of the traditional forty or more. If the job is freshly looked at, it may be that the formal skill and experience required for it are not so great as had previously been assumed.

At present the pressure from trade unions and professional bodies is nearly all the other way, since certified skill is a marketable commodity which its owners are not going to abandon without exacting the highest possible price. In Britain, for example, there have been disputes about the involvement of non-lawyers in house conveyancing. In the USA conveyancing is done cheaply and expeditiously by non-legal firms. Trade unions, similarly, have conducted bitter strikes to maintain the monopoly rights of their members over particular areas of work, ostensibly on craft grounds, although the actual skill content of the job may be largely notional. As the general level of skill required for many jobs declines, there is a natural tendency on the part of organized bodies of workers in such jobs to protect members' living standards by claiming and defending and insisting on being paid for skills which are no longer in use.

At the same time there is an increasing division of jobs into narrow specialities demanding particular qualifications which makes it difficult for people to change jobs without laborious and sometimes unnecessary re-training.

In the teaching profession, for example, which was previously open to all university graduates, there is now a requirement that all teachers, whether graduates or not, must have a teaching qualification which in the case of a graduate involves an extra year's study. Unquestionably the extra qualification is in general desirable. But the rigid insistence on it in all circumstances now makes it impossible to employ the graduate who might have a great deal to contribute in teaching his subject for a limited period but cannot take a year off to acquire the extra qualification.

To an ever-increasing extent, and for reasons more to do with maintaining earnings than with raising professional standards, work is being carved up into a multiplicity of narrow specialities for which the entrance fee is a separate paper qualfication. While some of these may be justified, their cumulative effect is to impede movement between different jobs at a time when changes in the economy require increasing numbers of workers to change industries, skills or occupations in mid-career.

Increasing specialization may make good economic sense in a number of jobs, but it can sometimes be harmful to the worker who is forced into a job with narrow horizons. The narrower the specialization, the more important it becomes in human terms that the worker does not have to devote his whole working life to it. If work is to become more specialized, this must be balanced by an increase in the adaptability of the worker. It must be made easier, not harder, for him to change jobs and acquire new skills.

If Multipurpose Man is to flourish, there must also be a change in society's attitudes to competition in work. 'Getting on' and 'getting ahead' in the rat-race have continuously been held up before us as desirable objectives. Except in politics, where 'careerist' is a term of abuse, the worker is exhorted to strive for promotion, the young executive is urged to lose no time in climbing the career ladder, the administrator is expected to intrigue for an ever larger empire to administer. A man's worth is all too frequently measured by his wealth, his power and his current earnings.

Among most factory and manual workers this urge to compete

seems to have made surprisingly little headway. Trade union habits of thought encourage the solidarity of a working group, and the struggle to advance economically is pursued by means of wage claims on behalf of whole sections of workers rather than by individual promotion. It is quite common for a worker to refuse promotion to charge-hand or foreman because this will cut him off from his mates. The worker making a big effort to get on is certainly not unknown, but his ambition is not generally admired by his workmates. He is despised as a crawler and gains no respect for his efforts.

In the business and professional world of managers, executives, salesmen and administrators, however, it is another story. The business community's jobs depend on their competing vigorously with other firms in the same trade. It is natural that this competitive spirit should be equally strong inside the firm. The thrusting qualities that enable an area manager to beat the firm's outside competition enable the same man to move upwards in his own firm. Some of these qualities—energy, imagination, shrewdness, judgment—are admirable. But they may be allied to—sometimes overridden by—the less admirable and socially less acceptable qualities of ruthless selfishness, inhumanity, dishonesty and cruelty. In a great many jobs as much of an executive's energies are devoted to advancing his own interests inside his firm as to coping with the outside opposition or simply getting on with the job.

Only in recent years has there developed a significant revolt against the competitive, inhuman pressures of the commercial rat-race. There has been a steady but growing trickle of men and women who have left the pursuit of highly competitive careers to work in more human conditions at a less frenetic and pressure-laden pace away from the big centres. An advertising chief gives up a top job to devote himself to charity work. An accountant leaves a City firm to set up practice in a farming area. Fleet Street journalists retire to write books in Cornwall. The movement is not large because the opportunities to earn even a more modest living in the peaceful byways are few. But there is certainly enough disenchantment with the rat-race to suggest that most people do not really want to earn their livings in an atmosphere of continual cut-throat competition and would be glad to break free from it if they knew how.

Multipurpose Man embodies a concept which cuts across many traditional attitudes to work and the worker. He needs a general acceptance of new attitudes if he is to prosper. At the same time, as he establishes himself on the employment scene, he will help to form new public attitudes more in keeping with the needs and aspirations of today's workers.

The man with two jobs frequently entering new spheres of activity cannot thrive if part-time work is despised and all the most interesting and rewarding work is reserved for those prepared to give it lifelong loyalty. But the determination of skilled and valued workers to give any one employer only part of their time could win increased respect for the part-timer.

Multipurpose Man needs to break down the division between activity to earn a living, work, from which little interest or fulfilment can be expected, and activity which the worker positively enjoys or finds fulfilling, leisure. He must learn to find many of the rewards and interests of leisure in work and treat some of his leisure interests as seriously as a job of work, to be given adequate time instead of crowded into odd evenings when he is tired. Society must be prepared to pay him adequately for the contribution he makes, whether it is in the field of traditionally paid work or in what is at present designated voluntary work.

Society must also accept new attitudes towards skill, loyalty, experience and competition. The man with two jobs is likely today to be regarded as insufficiently serious to be given responsibility by an employer. He will have to show that a refusal to sell his full working time to any one employer need not prevent his making a serious contribution when he is at work. He may even demonstrate that a man who refuses to get stale on the job may have an extra zest and freshness to offer.

None of the traditional attitudes to work are likely to change overnight, though in a period of rapid social change they may not prove so immutable as they seem today. But Multipurpose Man does not plan an overnight revolution either. Many workers will get much of the benefit of the new approach to work without changing their present way of working at all. One of the benefits of a working world in which each man writes his own work programme is a sense of liberation from the prison of factory or office. Freedom does not have to be exercised to be enjoyed. The knowledge that it exists for the taking is often enough to produce a sense of liberation.

What is important is that the door should be unlocked and be seen to be unlocked. It is not necessary to go through it every five minutes. There will always be many workers who by temperament and inclination would rather stay in one place that suits them and give all their activity time to it. There will be nothing to stop their carrying on as before if that is what they want. But they will not be under economic pressure to do so and they will be able to change to part-time work or another job whenever it suits them.

The younger workers are already demanding change and a limited commitment. Because few employers will give them worthwhile half-time jobs, they leave jobs frequently when they feel the need of a change and use frequent absenteeism to make the job fit their private arrangements. An employer who welcomes part-time workers as equal in status to full-timers may well secure more loyal, reliable and longer-term service from the men and women with limited commitments. They may not stay for life but they are more likely to give the job some useful years if they can see a clear way out.

Chapter three

Now you see them— now you don't

In a society organized on a one-man-one-job basis, and failing to achieve that aim, there is a surprising number of busy people already working at more than one job. Employers, trade union leaders and bureaucrats would rather have us neatly docketed once for all as tinker, tailor, soldier or sailor. Yet in spite of the barriers of practical difficulty, financial penalty and prejudice, a substantial minority at all levels and in many different fields of work already spread their energies and talents around among two or more jobs. To do so at present they often have to work much longer hours than would be acceptable in any one job. Some do so from financial necessity as the only way of earning enough to meet their commitments. But for many others the main motivation is not so much economic as the satisfactions they find in the life of the two-job man or woman.

All these multi-jobbers show what can be achieved in the face of a society which finds them a nuisance and an embarrassment and views them often with varying degrees of disapproval. Most of them suffer the severe disadvantage that one of their two or more jobs is a full-time one, even if not a fully satisfying one. To keep both jobs going they must work fatiguing hours and sacrifice time needed for recreation and rest. Some of them also sacrifice leisure, but the sacrifice here is less than might appear if the second job gives the satisfactions of a leisure activity, as it sometimes does. It is characteristic of some double-jobbers that they give to a leisure activity the disciplined dedication that others associate only with work; and they frequently get more satisfaction from it as a result.

Today's growing band of multi-jobbers falls into a number of loose and overlapping categories, in each of which the motives and the satisfaction may be different. In the top category financially are the bosses and the high establishment figures. For them money is not a worry or a motive for over-working, but the energies that took them to the top seldom allow them to

32

confine themselves to one employment when they get there.

Prime ministers, presidents, archbishops and military chiefs may find enough continuing variety and challenge in their jobs to absorb all the working energy they have. For top civil servants, business-men, and some trade union chiefs, however, the job itself is seldom enough. Once a man has reached the top of his particular ladder he can expect to have acquired a whole series of part-time jobs to prevent his feeling lonely or under-employed in his rarefied eminence. Commissions, committees and councils will compete for his membership. Professional, business and voluntary bodies will clamour for his services as speaker or fund-raiser. He will be asked to lecture, write books, become a television personality and give advice on innumerable matters. Only if he is exceptionally strong-minded will he be able to give as much as half his time to the job he is paid for.

When they retire, and sometimes long before they retire, these eminent figures will have opportunities to extend their interests by directorships or part-time membership of the boards of state industries. If they still have energies to spare, there are the hospital management boards and the governing councils of prestigious charities, educational bodies and research foundations. Even this is not enough to mop up the energies of some tycoons. One industrialist will relax by running a vineyard at a respectable profit, another will breed pedigree cattle, a third run a string of racehorses and a fourth absent-mindedly make a spare-time million or two in property speculation by way of unwinding from the serious business of running an international oil company. When you've battled your single-minded way to the top, work may be the only relaxation you know and every fun occupation turns into a business opportunity you can't resist. At the top of the achievement tree nobody doubts that his own experience, advice, flair and decision-taking expertise are valid in a wide variety of situations. At this level society is happy to accept that half a lifetime of wheeling and dealing or government in-fighting makes a man infinitely and all-embracingly wise.

A second category readily accepted in a multipurpose role is that of the artists and communicators. Painters, writers, musicians, television personalities, sculptors, actors, poets and the like are not expected by society to devote themselves to one particular job or to regular hours of work. It is accepted as part of the creative process for the artist, though not for a factory worker, to refuse to be tied down by discipline or industrious habits. Painters like Modigliani,

33

well known to have been drunk or drugged a good deal of the time, the mentally disturbed Van Gogh or the runaway Gauguin, are popularly supposed to have been in some way more genuinely artistic artists than those who live quiet lives and get on with their painting. The untidy, unorganized life is a guarantee of authenticity.

There is a popular prejudice against artists earning a steady living from their art. This is held to be evidence that they have sold their souls to mammon. In the popular view they should be needy enough to require another job besides their art, but not sufficiently disciplined actually to do one. It is socially admired for an artist to struggle against the financial odds by earning a living on the side but it counts as a black mark against his artistic integrity if he does so too successfully.

These romantic notions aside, however, creative workers have always been among the most adaptable and assiduous of double-jobbers. Their creative urge has usually impelled them to seek new challenges and new ways of using their talents, while economic necessity has made them resourceful in combining paid work with unprofitable but necessary artistic freedom. In many cases different ways of using creative talents are desirable and welcomed for their own sake. The painter who teaches part time at an art school may not only be glad of the regular money, he may also welcome the chance to communicate his knowledge and enthusiasm and perhaps derive some stimulation from his students. Writers and poets have often been happy to apply their skills to commercial tasks and have often quite cheerfully combined writing with office work. The poet Dylan Thomas was not only glad of the money when commissioned to write a film script for an oil company; he welcomed the interest of the trip abroad and the technical challenge involved. T. S. Eliot in his bank and later his publishing office was only one of many poets to give poetry the dedication of a serious job of work while retaining and valuing a place in the workaday office community. Novelists frequently not only need the regular income that part-time reviewing or work quite unconnected with writing can bring; they need also the social contacts which bring relief from one of the loneliest occupations in the world.

Few creative workers can be creative all the time. If their finances permit it, they may take time off to travel, to meet people, to seek new experiences, to think or read or simply let the mind lie fallow. But if they are not so fortunately placed as to be able to do this, or even if they are, they may find equal value from the point of view of variety and the recharging of creative batteries in doing a non-creative job, possibly quite unconnected with their creative talent. A man cut off from the working world is a man cut off from life, and few creative people gain from this. All too familiar in literature is the writer who produces a best-selling novel about the working life he knows, comes to the big city to be a full-time writer and soon runs out of the first-hand experience his talent needs.

Spare-time musicians usually need the extra money but in this case the distinction between work and leisure is often blurred beyond definition. The printer, the insurance man, the office worker and the plumber who play together at evening engagements may need to do so but are glad to be making music anyway. They are getting more enjoyment and relaxation out of it than most men do from their unpaid stint on the golf course. And they put more disciplined skill into it than many men do in highly paid career jobs.

Actors, again, take other jobs from financial need endemic in a notoriously underemployed profession. Modelling, running shops, writing books or cleaning houses all help to keep actors eating between engagements. Yet here, too, economics are not everything. There is a need for change even when it is not dictated by necessity; it may be demanded by the spirit. The successful actor in a long-running play may want to leave the cast once it no longer offers an artistic challenge to him. Variety is necessary for artistic as well as for financial health.

In the professions variety of employment arises naturally from the nature of the work. The lawyer may stick to his profession but in the course of a single working day he may apply himself to the quite separate and different problems of half a dozen clients. His work may take him to conferences anywhere between a palace and a prison, but even if he stays in his own office he may be called upon to give his mind to such diverse matters as a divorce, a property deal, a case of shoplifting, a complicated will or maladministration in a government department. Not only this but his clients, too, are as diverse in character as their problems. The lawyer in a partnership has no boss. He is responsible to himself for what he does and how he organizes his work. As a member of a profession he has independence, variety, changing interests, all the qualities that make a job an absorbing occupation instead of wage-slavery or a repetitive chore. He is also well placed to pursue, if he wishes, other interests unconnected with the law. A solicitor like Lord Goodman, who at various times combined his law practice with being an active chairman of the

35

Arts Council and confidential negotiator with the rebel Rhodesian regime, was only one highly publicized example of many professional men with a wide variety of active interests.

Doctors, surgeons, accountants, vicars, civil engineers, architects and scientists of many kinds can similarly organize their lives to provide the maximum of independence and variety, and many of them do. In many ways the professional man, as an independent principal, has the ideal working arrangement. He is in full charge of his working life. He need take bullying from no one. His qualifications ensure his self-respect and the respect of the community. His status is assured, to a large extent independently of the size of his earnings. He can work hard or coast along, varying the pace by his own decision. And because his special qualifications are respected in fields other than his own, he often finds it easier than most to turn to another field of work altogether if he wishes. Not only can a Lord Goodman apply his lawyer's skills to Central African politics, but a country clergyman can produce a best-selling book of plant drawings, a doctor can become a famous novelist, playwright or television producer, a civil engineer, a designer of jewellery.

Other people are similarly many-sided in their interests and in their potential for personal development, but few are so well equipped to move from one field of interest to another. The professional man can do so more easily not only because of his independent status but also because his specialist training inculcates knowledge, habits of thought and self-discipline which are applicable in fields far away from his speciality.

Politicians and voluntary workers of all kinds form another category of those who have already taken to the multipurpose way of life. Politicians may have their special interests and particular skills but they are almost by definition jacks of a number of different trades. Except for a few sons of political families sent to Eton and Oxford with a political career in mind, they are not trained from the start for politics. It is usually something people get into, from discovered aptitude or acquired interest, after starting to earn a living at something else. Even when the politician has become a professional by getting elected to the House of Commons or Congress he can still find himself, after the next election, looking for work in some other trade.

Politics themselves, as the science of government and the practical pursuit of power, can involve their devotees in every conceivable kind of business or field of activity. If the business of America is

36

business, as President Coolidge remarked, it is equally true that business of all kinds is the business of the politician. In political life itself there is ample scope for the pursuit of a wide enough variety of interests to satisfy the most restless spirit. But if this is not enough, it is approved for a British Member of Parliament to keep up, if he can, whatever business or professional interests he had before being elected. Though increasingly bogged down in the technicalities of politics, an MP is still regarded, at least in theory, as a part-timer who spends his afternoons and evenings in Parliament while taking his doctor's surgery, arguing cases in court, running his business, writing his books, acting as consultant or public relations man or performing on television in his own time. The expertise and know-ledge of the world he gains from his outside occupation, it is reck-oned, helps to make him a more knowledgeable and useful MP.

The paid professional politician, however, is a member of a small, privileged minority in the political world. The vast majority of those active in politics, in town councils and on ward committees, are unpaid and are under the necessity of earning a living however busy their political lives may be. Thus it is not unknown for the mayor of a British city, with enough civic duties and ceremonies to keep any man fully employed for a year, to do a day's work driving a locomo-tive and then change out of his overalls into his ceremonial robes before entertaining some of his recent passengers. Adaptability and wide interests are part of the politician's stock-in-trade. Without the frequent changes and contrasts in his activities many an unpaid, spare-time politician would find the strain of overwork too much for him.

The same is true of many other voluntary workers who put in after their paid working hours a very active part-time stint, no less skilled and demanding for being self-chosen and self-disciplined. Many valuable charities doing essential work for the homeless, the sick, the unfortunate and the deprived would find it impossible to carry on without the work of devoted people who have in effect taken on two demanding jobs, though getting paid only for one. Charities used to rely on middle and upper class ladies of leisure who needed an escape from idleness but this source is rapidly shrinking as more wives demand and win the right to work.

A final category of people to whom the holding of more than one job comes naturally is that of academics and teachers. Teaching at all levels involves the communication of knowledge and the stimulation of thought. It would be a poor teacher, or perhaps a tired one, who considered that his salary-based duties in the lecture-hall or class-room, together with the study, preparation and other work associated with a formal teaching job, absorbed all he had to give. The professor on television and the journalist don are familiar media men. Some school teachers earn substantial sums from the writing of school textbooks. Many in the teaching profession lecture on their special subjects. All these activities may be considered as teaching carried on by other means, involving various applications of their particular professional skill and knowledge. All this has a value greatly in excess of the purely financial benefits. The wider use of teaching skills in different forms keeps the teacher fresher and more in touch with the world and improves his techniques to the benefit of his pupils as well as enriching society in general.

But the technique of teaching is not the only area in which the teacher has a contribution to make outside the process of formal instruction. A teacher must have some skill or knowledge to impart, and in many cases the practice of his skill in the outside world, or the application of his special knowledge, provides a completely separate field in which he can exercise his talents and earn money. Long school holidays make this easier for teachers than for most other workers.

Many teachers already manage to confine their teaching to two or three days a week, leaving themselves free to work at something else for the rest of the week. But even those who teach full time are still able to build up quite substantial second careers.

Typical of these is the head of music at a London school who is also a busy freelance broadcaster on musical subjects. He enjoys both careers: teaching stimulates him and he is happy as a broadcaster because he can enjoy the interest of the job without the worry of relying on it for a living. He finds that broadcasting helps his teaching because it widens his knowledge; teaching helps his broadcasting because it makes him explain things simply to a non-specialist audience. For an individual of these particular talents and interests the double-job arrangement is a means of gaining maximum fulfilment in life. However, it can be tiring, since he is often at work through weekends and has to put in very long days during the week. He would prefer to work half time at each job if there were any half-time teaching jobs of equivalent status to the one he now has.

These categories of people to whom double-jobbing comes naturally are only a minority of those who already do two jobs. In many other jobs, in which it is not nearly so easy or so convenient, workers

38

feel impelled to do something else on the side. Though they are sometimes lumped together as double-jobbers or moonlighters they differ widely in their motives for taking on extra work. It is possible to identify a number of different reasons for double-jobbing, although many individuals have, of course, more than one reason.

The most common, most compelling and least satisfactory reason for taking on a second job is to earn more money. All too often this is an unskilled job, badly paid, especially if moonlighters form a major part of the work-force. If they are already in full-time jobs they are not so likely to be militant about pay in their part-time jobs, though their potential striking force, if efficiently organized, is actually greater in the second job than in the full-time one. Part-time evening jobs for moonlighters—driving minicabs, waiting in restaurants, restocking supermarkets and many others—usually offer little except money, and not very much of that.

Some of the more skilled moonlighting jobs, on the other hand, while offering better pay for the effort involved, are in effect simply extensions of the main job for different employers or for oneself. Thus an employee of a firm of electrical contractors may spend his evenings doing private electrical work. Nearly all those who do second jobs need the extra money, but if extra money is the only reason for the extra job it can soon become a depressing burden.

There are many other powerful reasons besides the need for money which impel people to take up second jobs. One is the boredom of an unsatisfying job and the need to find elsewhere some of the ingredients of satisfaction which the first job lacks.

One man motivated in this way was a correspondent in East St Louis, Illinois, who responded to an invitation to double-jobbers to describe the satisfaction and drawbacks of this way of life. He worked as a salesman and demonstrator by day and, after four hours' sleep, worked all night as a railroad freight car brake inspector. His railroad job, he wrote, offered absolutely no challenge but he felt he could not leave because it carried fringe benefits such as life insurance and sick benefits for his family that had taken years to accumulate. Work as a salesman also lacked the challenge he sought, so he gave that up and took a college course in business administration and tax form preparation. At the time of writing he was practising from his home as a licensed notary public and tax consultant during the day and still working for the railroad at night. The body seemed to be just a little tired most of the time, he admitted, but the second job gave him a sense of accomplishment which satisfied his

personal drive and an increase in social prestige, which was important to him.

The railroad notary public illustrates also a second motivation for
moonlighting, the ambition to be one's own boss. This is one of the
most powerful of all motivations for double-jobbing because for
many people it represents the only practical avenue of advancement.
For these people the real goal is not immediate financial gain but the
independence and personal security which even a well-paid employee
can never have.

The independence of the small businessman, who has built up a
personal business by being a bit more hard-working than his neighbour, has long been a prized and socially admired American goal. It
accords well with the traditional American dream of a society in
which every barefoot lad from a log-cabin can make it to the top by
hard work. Double-jobbing can make the dream a reality because
little or no capital is required to get started. The main job pays the
rent and feeds the family while the spare-time sales agent, toy manu-
facturer, car repairer or boutique owner is getting the business off the
ground. The same motivation is gaining ground in Britain though the
one-man business does not yet enjoy the same social admiration.

The urge to be one's own boss often goes with a strong moral urge
towards self-improvement. This was illustrated by a correspondent
in Nebraska who worked a nine-hour day in a factory and did selling
and repair work in his spare time. In a letter to me he wrote: 'Recently I have reasoned that I can offer much more to my community by offering my services during off-hours. . . . I must hold
service foremost and let the reward follow.' He was confident of
considerable development in his range of spare-time services, he
said, because Christian Science had taught him that there was no
limit to man's abilities.

The yearning for independence, the need not to be beholden to
any boss who can order one's life, runs through many letters from
double-jobbers. It does not have to take the form of full self-
employment. As one writer pointed out, a valuable form of independence is won simply by having more than one employer. This
man, living in New York, was fired from his job as a mechanic at
the age of fifty.

'The twenty-eight years at this occupation,' he wrote in a letter
to me,

'had fashioned me into an hourly paid worker who was

gradually ground down to accept as normal a supervisor over-seeing my work, a place on a seniority roster and to feel that I must hang on for dear life to this job because we were always being reminded that we're getting old and we could not do any-thing else. The overseers . . . never missed an opportunity to humiliate you and to make you feel insignificant. . . . '

After much trouble he succeeded in getting part-time work maintain-ing the pinsetting machines at three different bowling alleys, and dis-covered that an employer trebled was practically no employer at all. He recalled:

'I had found it very miserable to try to make out in one estab-lishment when business was falling apart. You could not earn a good week's wages without a good deal of resentment on the operator's part. Why not take on part-time jobs in several places and guarantee each operator trouble-free operation, especially if you kept yourself available for emergency? Working for three places, I was able to earn close to two hundred dollars a week. I insisted on keys to the places so that I could work as needed and I set the hours and days in the week when I would do preventive maintenance in each place. It worked just fine. It was like work-ing for myself. I did not have to take any orders from anyone. . . . They never bothered me and I never felt under pressure from anyone.'

A woman correspondent in Rhode Island noted that 'a full-time job brings the demands of loyalty and devotion. It can require overtime work not rewarded and reduces one to a slave.' She saw the effect in her own family:

'My husband worked fifteen years for one company when they retired him. Since then he has fallen into the same trap of work-ing exclusively for one concern. He is just as tired and bored as when he worked for the first place. I don't believe this applies to the young and enthusiastic worker. But around middle age, beginning at forty, one does look back and wonder if most of one's life was spent wisely.'

Ideally, she wrote, two jobs should be totally different from one another. Three or four days indoors, two days outdoors. Or three days at a computer, two days' carpentry or painting houses. The

41

yearning for freedom, the itch to break out of the rut before life has run out, is a powerful one.

There are those who take second jobs in order to maintain old skills as well as earn extra money. A British firm estimated that between fifteen and twenty per cent of its shift process workers had spare-time jobs. Many of these, the firm estimated, were ex-tradesmen who joined the company as unskilled or semi-skilled men, attracted by the high rates of pay. Their spare-time jobs were connected with their old trades of carpentry, plumbing, bricklaying, interior decorating, etc., and it was thought that they wanted to keep up these skills for possible future use.

A Colorado woman with a master's degree in psychology, as well as a small family, devised a working life involving four paid part-time jobs so that she could use her existing skills, acquire new ones, earn good money and help her husband. She had a part-time job as an audio-visual consultant, for which her psychology degree was relevant. She worked as required as vocational counsellor for a guidance clinic. This only amounted to eight hours or less a month but she wrote: 'That hardly seems worth the bother but it has very tangible benefits for me. As a "housewife" I have no professional identity. But as a vocational counsellor I do. I retain the sense of staying in a field I once worked at full-time.'

This busy woman helped as a book-keeper in her husband's small business and about four times a year worked on a skilled technical film job for the local television station. Her job as audio-visual consultant, in which she used a small video-tape to record counsellors in training in interviews so that they can watch themselves and improve their techniques, gave her particular satisfaction. She explained:

> 'Although I have the job because we need the money ... it allows me to explore an entirely new field which is tremendously exciting to me. . . . Ever since college I have had a dual background of psychology (counselling) and television-film. They never fit together. Now I have a way to use them both, which gives my life some sense, even though my time is very broken up.'

Her fifth part-time job was unpaid, she said. It involved 'mothering a three-year-old boy, wifing a thirty-nine-year-old husband, cooking and shopping, washing and ironing and cleaning house for a family of three. . . . I think it will be the women who pioneer the part-time job because their lives are fragmented by the demands of society.'

A mother of five in Rhode Island put the point more contentedly: 'Having worked at the necessary diversified home duties plus outside church and other volunteer work for twenty years, I cannot be truly happy unless I am busy at two or more jobs now that the family is almost grown.' Besides running her home she was studying for a music degree at a local college and working three afternoons a week teaching piano, recorder and singing.

For many in boring or restricted jobs and for homebound wives the pleasure of meeting people can be a powerful incentive to do an extra job. It is undoubtedly a more powerful attraction than money for many who go out to do housework for others. To many daily helps the interest of gossiping with another wife and keeping up with all the family's business is an important part of the payment. A South London woman wrote to say that she gave up a boring office job to work part-time as caretaker for a small block of flats and as part-time assistant in her husband's off-licence partly because she wanted to meet people, which she does in both jobs in a way that allows her to chat with them, and partly because she wanted to spend more time with her husband.

One further possible motive for some of today's moonlighters, especially in America, is suggested by a young woman sociologist in Colorado. After taking a master's degree she worked part-time as university instructor in sociology and worked at a second job as a checker-out at a discount store. The two jobs were diametrically opposed, one being highly intellectual and the other involving almost no mental effort. 'The two jobs were complementary,' she wrote, 'in that each made me respect the other. The manual job made me understand how a large segment of our population exists.' Even though the manual job was something of an exercise in self-discipline, she found doing the two jobs more interesting than a previous spell of full-time teaching. She added: 'I have a strong feeling that the amount of work performed in forty hours could often be condensed to twenty hours, allowing an equal amount of time for a second activity.'

This writer was about to start a full-time job, yet she knew she would take on extra work as well, 'not so much for financial supplements but more of a psychological supplement. It is conceivable that many people who do second jobs do so to fill a psychological need which may reflect a need for a re-evaluation of the actual role of work in our society.' This psychological need, she thought, might derive from the typical American's inability to handle leisure time:

43

'Often I feel the second job is more of a cover-up for this uneasiness with extra time.'

She may well be right. A full-time worker doing a spare-time job, either paid or voluntary, may simply be filling in a void, perhaps because of an inability to relax or in response to a feeling that idleness is sin. Most of the people who do two jobs today do so from a combination of reasons of which money is not necessarily the dominant one. Even when part-time working in itself carries no social status very many people feel a powerful urge to take it up. For many of these people some variety is a necessity and a second job provides a liberating outlet, even when considerable physical and practical difficulties are put in the way. If these difficulties were removed, a working variety might well be sought by many more.

Chapter four

A new kind of man

For various reasons a large number of men and women, estimated as something like sixteen per cent of Britain's labour force, is already working at two paid jobs or at part-time jobs which give an opportunity to do other things during the working week. These men and women have found advantage in doing two jobs, even though society is not organized for versatility. While they have found two jobs personally helpful, therefore, they have had to endure a number of disadvantages which could be eliminated if multiple part-time working were the norm.

The most obvious disadvantage of the two-job man today is that almost invariably he has to pay for his satisfactions with exhaustion. Since few are able to organize two part-time jobs, most have had to work at a part-time as well as a full-time job. A few have even held two full-time jobs at once. Only very rarely today is a man able to split a normal working week among two jobs.

The second major disadvantage of part-time work today is its generally low status. There are part-time chairmen and board members at the top and part-time consultancies in the professions. But most part-time employment available today is for routine clerical, service, delivery or manual jobs. Part-time skilled work is hard to come by and part-time management at junior and middle levels is almost unheard of.

The shortage of full-time jobs is a complicating factor. As long as it persists, older workers in particular will be reluctant to venture outside the security of existing jobs and any form of job mobility becomes more difficult. It will be hard enough for a man to get one job, let alone two. The choice of jobs available will be very limited for everybody and the choice of part-time jobs of reasonable status in any one location will be very small if it exists at all. In some centres badly hit by unemployment, talk of double jobs will sound like a bad joke.

However, none of these drawbacks is necessarily permanent. All of

45

them can be overcome if industry and society are determined that they shall be. Adequate employment, in particular, must be provided if *any* healthy and stable society is to thrive. So let us suppose that these disadvantages are eliminated.While retaining the position in which a man can work at one job all his life if he prefers, let us suppose that conditions have been created in which anybody who wants to can work at two part-time jobs as readily as at one full-time job; that part-time jobs are available at all levels of status and skill and the employee can please himself. If he wants to work full-time, fine. But if he would rather work part-time, that too can be arranged even at skilled, high-status level. If he wishes, he can work half the week at one job, half at another, choosing similar or contrasting jobs or any combination for which he has the necessary skills. How would this situation help the worker? What benefits would it bring?

It would first of all provide a blessed escape from the prison of boredom in which millions are serving life sentences. 'For most manual workers and for growing numbers of white-collar workers, work is a boring, monotonous, even painful experience,' said Mr. Roy Jenkins MP in a speech at Leicester in June 1972. He was enunciating a truth which workers know all too well but which is seldom acknowledged by politicians. Efforts have been made by some far-sighted industrialists, notably by Volvo, the Swedish car manufac-turers, to rearrange assembly-line work to reduce the boredom. Even when this is possible, it is a palliative rather than a cure. Some of the humanity which has been designed out of the job by the apostles of scientific management can be designed in again by the industrial psychologists. But not, in the end, a great amount. Putting things to-gether in a team and varying the sequence from time to time is better than tightening nuts on a moving track all day. But it still does not amount to a job that challenges the mind.

Cutting the job in half would more than cut the boredom in half. Boredom arises from repetition and a sense that what is being done involves no problem, makes no challenge and demands no alertness. The feeling builds up in the course of a day spent at a repetitive job and becomes more intense the longer the working day goes on. It accumulates during the week and over the years until a man comes to hate the grinding tyranny of the assembly line. For the first few hours of the day a certain amount of interest may be sustained, when mind and body are fresh. There are private and social matters to think about and no great effort of will is needed to keep the body at its task. Up to a point it can even be pleasant as well as profitable to work at a well-paid assembly line job. It can offer relaxation from thought and outside worries; it can provide a soothing rhythm and a sense of something being done. For a short time these can be satisfactions.

If nobody had to work forty hours a week on the assembly line, if a twenty-hour part-time stint was normal, there would be much less than half as much boredom. Half-time work would never go on long enough for tedium to start accumulating. There would be time for it to disperse before the next stint.

Equally, half-time working could put an end to boredom's companion, exhaustion. Many assembly-line workers have admitted that at the end of a shift they are too tired to enjoy a life of their own. They have energy left only to go home, watch television, perhaps go out for a beer. They are in no condition for anything that demands thought, social effort or active physical movement. Exhaustion, too, builds up over the weeks and over the years. The assembly-line worker, paced by the machine, has not recovered his vigour by rest and recreation before he has to go to work again the next day. Many jobs are physically taxing and the middle-aged man, in particular, finds that he cannot keep up a pace set for young men.

As a worker gets past his youth, part-time working makes sense for physically demanding jobs. It makes sense for employers at all times, since exhaustion leads to lower output. Even today, when the cost of employing two workers part-time is marginally higher than the cost of one full-time worker, employers have found that increased output and reduced absenteeism more than compensate for the higher labour cost.

Indeed, the elimination of stress from both boredom and fatigue which part-time working brings to the factory must result in substantial benefits in better time-keeping, drastically reduced absenteeism and a fall in the number of working days lost through sickness and strikes. A considerable amount of absenteeism and lateness can be attributed to fatigue, which contributes also to ill-health. This is another factor, with boredom, in the escalation of work disputes into strikes.

So far fatigue and boredom have been considered as they affect employees at operating level. At managerial level there should certainly be less boredom, since the manager's function is, or should be, a problem-solving one. But in situations in which he has to cope with a great many problems he may well work longer hours than the man on the shop

47

floor and suffer just as much from mental and physical fatigue.

He may also suffer considerably from stresses of anxiety about the job and its problems and about competition for status and promotion within the firm. If the lack of problems to solve can cause boredom amounting to physical deterioration, too many problems to solve too continuously can cause anxieties which bring on ulcers. This is not exclusively a management condition, of course. London bus drivers operating all day in heavy traffic are as much prone to ulcers as anxious executives.

Among many people in jobs subject to heavy stress there is now a growing revulsion against the conditions in which such jobs have traditionally been carried on. In the business rat-race, executives, managers and salesmen are expected to drive themselves to the limit for the good of the company to gain high monetary rewards. The successful man may reach middle life with a relatively high material standard of living gained at the expense of his health, his peace of mind, his leisure and the quality of his life. Increasing numbers of young executives and professional men view this prospect as a poor bargain and opt out of it.

The process has been noted by a London University occupational psychologist, Roger Williams. He told a newspaper interviewer: 'Increasing numbers of middle class, middle management people no longer regard work as a central life interest. Promotions are being turned down. More university graduates are opting out of the industrial rat race and settling for a comfortable job well within their capabilities and allowing time to pursue leisure or sporting interests.' If there is a significant swing away from work by the middle classes, he considered, drastic changes will have to be made in our education system and indeed in our whole society. 'Much of the country's prosperity depends on the work involvement of such key individuals as executives, managers, engineers, scientists and professional people of all kinds.'

Mr Williams noted a growing realization of the mental and physical illness that can result from work stress and found among graduates and those already in industry a growing distaste for a competitive form of life. For such people the eventual rewards did not justify the efforts and sacrifices involved.

If too many talented and qualified people settle for easy options and turn down promotion, the effect on industry could be catastrophic. It may be doubted whether changes in the education system would do much good if these were directed towards reviving a flagging spirit of competitive overwork. The manpower crisis is likely to be all the more acute because the opters-out are likely to be among the more intelligent of managerial talent. For if management is largely a matter of weighing objectively the factors in a situation and deciding on a course most likely to achieve the desired end, those who have dropped out of the rat-race have probably displayed managerial talent of a high order in relation to their own goals of personal and family happiness. It is probably not their education that needs to be changed; rather that industry needs to be adapted to offer an acceptable life to the people on whom its future prosperity depends.

A part-time commitment is one possible answer. It would attack simultaneously both the stress on the individual and the distasteful competitive element of business and industrial life. An executive, a scientist or a manager faced only with the alternatives of dedicating virtually his whole life to a job of high stress content or getting out into calmer waters may well opt for the quieter life. He will do so the more readily at a time when the quieter life is still an available option if he sees colleagues who have opted for the stress and the bigger rewards displaced by take-overs or failing in health in middle age, when it may be much more difficult to make a new start.

The same man may well be happy to take on a demanding job if it is not a full-time commitment. The challenging and stretching of the mind can be invigorating and enjoyable provided they are not carried to the point of stress and fatigue. Taking on a part-time commitment, the executive allows his talents and skills to be developed by being tested to the full; they will not, however, be tested to destruction. If he takes another part-time job in a contrasted and more relaxed field he keeps himself in top mental shape for the challenges of the more demanding job. At the same time he improves the quality of his personal life, keeps fresh enough to enjoy family life and leisure pursuits and frees himself from the additional anxiety that some turn of industrial fortune beyond his control will one day destroy a job to which he has devoted his whole life.

It may be objected that the managerial jobs which at present are most subject to stress are precisely those which could not be done on a part-time basis. After all, part of the stress usually arises in the first place because the job is already more than a full-time one. Manager and scientist are faced with vast amounts of homework that have to be mastered before the right decisions can be taken.

It is all more than any one man can cope with in a sixty-hour week, let alone a dilettante's twenty hours or so.

Instead of re-educating the man to fit a highly-stressed job, the stress job must be re-designed to make it fit for a civilized man to do. Industrial pyschologists have spent a good deal of time re-designing repetitive jobs on the factory floor to make them team operations in which small groups can work together, giving each other support and taking a collective pride and satisfaction. Outstanding improvements are claimed for this reorganization in terms of job satisfaction, industrial harmony and increased efficiency. It is possible that the factors which have been found to make the factory floor job more agreeable could also be applied beneficially in the executive offices. It may be that managerial staffs would work better and with less stress as genuinely cooperative teams instead of as a series of small personal empires, each the responsibility of one man.

Teamwork is most highly developed in situations like the moonshots, where innumerable decisions have to be taken on a round-the-clock basis. There is no room here for a second-class control team functioning simply to keep things going until the top men come in to take the major decisions. Fresh, alert thinking has to be available at all times. Since no master-mind can stay in master-mind form twenty-four hours a day for long periods, shifts of duty control teams have to be employed who can come on fresh, take whatever decisions are needed as they come up and go home to relax before they begin to suffer from fatigue. Air traffic control centres, army headquarters staffs and daily newspapers are also familiar with the concept of the duty executive whose functions are taken over by somebody else on a shift basis. There is no compelling reason why similar arrangements at management level should not be extended to allow part-time shifts.

Many of the stress jobs could be broken down in function as well as in time. In a big firm the management team may have executives responsible for works, planning, research, transport, finance, industrial relations, public relations, advertising, buying, sales, property and so on. In a smaller firm all these separate functions may be combined for management purposes into three or four departments. Yet in functional terms it may make as much sense to treat them separately in a small firm as in a large one. They have been grouped simply because one department does not provide a full-time job for an executive. Separating them again into their genuinely distinct functions will provide a number of responsible part-time jobs, reduce the stress

50

on any one executive and probably ensure that each function gets the fresh attention of an expert instead of the tired attention of an executive with too many other problems on his mind.

The philosophical change required might be more difficult to bring about than this purely mechanical redistribution of executive portfolios. A good deal of stress arises today from a doctrine of personal responsibility. Transport is John Smith's responsibility and if a delivery is late or goes astray it is a black mark against him unless he can prove it is someone else's fault, which he naturally sets out to do. Even if he does not pass the buck publicly, perhaps recognizing that this is a posture which can never be wholly dignified, he nevertheless seeks out and puts the fear of God into the guilty party privately to ensure that his department, and therefore his own standing, is not let down again. By this combination of fear and personal status-seeking, efficiency of a kind is maintained.

This sort of personal competition, in which the executive's own standing is necessarily more important to him and to his career prospects than the performance of the company as a whole, is an impediment to rational staffing. The more intelligent younger professionals are repelled by it, it causes stress, and it is almost certainly not the most effective way to solve a company's overall problems. For these reasons there is a strong case for instituting at executive level the sort of team thinking which has been found so beneficial on the factory floor. There is, of course, already much lip-service to team-work in management. The management team is a boring cliché associated with windy exhortations about the need for each man to pull his weight and not let the side down. But all too often the reality behind the rhetoric is individual empire-building and a competitive power hierarchy. This has to be broken down by loosening the rigid power structure and apportioning rewards, status and responsibility more on a group than an individual basis. There would then be some real incentive to practise cooperation instead of just talking about it. The result would be a genuinely relaxed atmosphere, genuine interdepartmental helpfulness and genuine loyalty to a working group whose members would not be seen as career competitors. In time, public attitudes would switch away from today's admiration and respect for the ruthless get-ahead rat-racer. The selfish careerist would come to be regarded as dangerously anti-social and a liability to the business.

Given this new approach to jobs of responsibility and potential stress, the part-timer would be able to fit happily into the management structure and make a welcome and respected contribution. The part-timer himself would not feel at a disadvantage in relation to full-time colleagues. Nor would his career prospects suffer from his limited commitment. He could contribute to group decisions and activities at all levels and take progressively greater responsibilities within a narrowed range. The part-time executive would be relaxed, free from stress and anxiety. He would be able to assess situations more objectively and be more independent in his outlook. Collectively the part-timers in a company would be able to bring to bear a first-hand, up-to-date knowledge of the outside world which could be a valuable asset.

A feeling of freedom and a freedom from fear, and therefore a new attitude to work, would be among the benefits of part-time working in a society in which this was a recognized and respected option. The part-timer would feel loyalty to the work-groups in which he spent portions of his working week but no one group would dominate his whole working life. He would not see any one group so frequently and continuously that its members got on his nerves. Nor would he enter into a relationship with a foreman or a supervisor in which he depended on one man for the favour of continued employment. The part-time worker would be, and would feel himself to be, a free man with self-respect and dignity who would cooperate with colleagues to get a job done but who could not be bullied because he was not fully in any man's economic power. The supervisor would realize this and the old-style bullying foreman, already an obsolescent figure, would disappear. In his place would appear the coordinator of the team, leading instead of driving, treating his working colleagues with respect.

This new relationship between employer and employed might take time to settle down harmoniously. In the early days of a two-job economy both sides would be feeling their way. The employee might overdo his freedom and the employer might resort too readily to dismissal in the absence of lesser disciplinary sanctions. But a genuinely cooperative, non-authoritarian atmosphere would soon be established in which productivity would rise, disciplinary problems decline and personal relationships could flourish without the constraints of dependence, hierarchy or fear. Probably labour turnover would rise but this would no longer be a result or a sign of bad industrial relations. Workers would leave simply because they felt like a change. They would not be bound by a semi-feudal loyalty to the company. Nor would they feel that they were leaving almost the whole of their social life behind them.

Problems created by an increase in labour turnover would be offset by the higher level of education of all workers and their higher motivation to think for themselves. To jobs which required skill and experience they would bring a better average intelligence, a fresh interest and a willingness and ability to learn fast. The two-job man would not only be more widely experienced than the average worker today; he would be more mature as a person and in his attitude to work. He would not see himself as a man settling into a job for life and working for a pension, a man who hopes he has made the last big decision of his life in taking the job. He would see himself as a man on the move, a man still in progress, going places. He would not see the current job as a life sentence. He would see it as a challenge to meet and master before moving on to something new, perhaps something more challenging.

Enterprise and change would come naturally to the two-job man. In leaving one job and starting another he would not be risking everything. There would still be his second job to keep him going if one venture proved unlucky. He would not be held back from a move by the thought that he could be ruining a career long worked and schemed for. Feeling under no oppressive stress at work, he would not be tempted to make a rash decision to move for no good reason, or simply to escape. But neither would he be constrained to stay in a job which had proved entirely uncongenial simply out of fear to make a change.

Many people make most of their social contacts at work. They are on first-name terms with more people at the factory, shop or office than in their home circle. They know their workmates better and often like them better than the neighbours, relations and pub acquaintances who form their social contacts away from work. There are advantages and disadvantages in this. It can be pleasant to be part of a working group in which all the members know each other well, but it can be embarrassing and confining if they know each other too well. A group can see so much of each other at work that they know all there is to know about each other. They are not away from each other long enough to enrich the pool of social experience with new thoughts or experiences. They have no new opinions, no new conversation, and they may well start boring each other after a time.

The two-job man has a built-in safeguard against this. He too has a social group of workmates he knows well enough to be on good terms with. He may have, in fact, two such groups. But with the members of neither group does he have an all-day relationship. While there are areas of his life he shares with his workmates, there are also areas of his life which are not subject to their detailed day-to-day scrutiny. Not only is he a man who can contribute experiences gathered elsewhere to his circle of workmates and so become a fresher, more interesting person to them; he also gains a measure of personal privacy. He can, if he wishes, keep part of himself to himself, not revealing his whole life and circumstances to all who work with him.

Many people will regard this as no great privilege; they thrive in a situation in which their lives are an open book and they are flattered if anybody bothers to read it. But there is another sort of worker who feels uncomfortably exposed in the crowd at work. He values some personal privacy and needs it for his peace of mind. Doing two jobs and splitting his working life between two sets of workmates enables him to achieve this. Modern society tends to strip more and more privacy away from the individual, leaving him socially naked with his vital statistics indecently exposed to any snooper. By keeping on the move between jobs he becomes harder to pin down.

By keeping some personal privacy, the two-job worker also manages to preserve and cultivate some individuality. The totally exposed personality can seldom become a real individual. Any individual tendencies he may have are known and can be eliminated by social pressure before they have time to take hold. The fully social, ever-exposed man is always under pressure to conform to the social usages and prejudices of his companions. Only through movement, keeping open ways of escape, can he become uniquely himself.

Everyone is shaped and conditioned by the way he works. Some are shaped into sheep, others are conditioned to be slaves. Many are driven into sullen discontent and aching resentment by the pressures, stresses and attitudes they encounter in their work. The man who works all his life at a boring, frustrating job becomes a bored, frustrated person. Not only at work but in his personality outside working hours he is stunted and immature, denied the growth of which he is capable. A man with narrow horizons at work may hope to compensate by a richly varied social and private life, and a few may do so. But he is more likely to be as narrow in his social outlook as in his work. People are creatures of habit, or can soon become so, and habits of thought and behaviour acquired at work are not as easily thrown off at home as working clothes.

Multipurpose Man, like everyone else, will be the product of his working environment. His habits of thought and his social attitudes will be strongly influenced by his habits of work. He will differ considerably from today's one-job man, and not only in his working arrangements. Though many of his attitudes cannot be predicted, some likely changes in his temperament can be foreseen.

He will almost certainly be a more pleasant person, more relaxing to be with, more considerate, less aggressive. This will be only partly because he will be less tired and bored and under no unmanageable work stress. He will have a different attitude to work. He will feel interest in it and want to do well at it. But it will be a cooler, more objective interest; work will not dominate his life or his thinking. His development as a person will be as important to him as his development as a man with a job.

The tendency to opt out of the rat-race, already noted, will in Multipurpose Man be developed to the point where he will not involve himself in it in the first place. He will be cooperative rather than competitive. In one sense he will take work more seriously than many who dedicate their lives to their careers: he will be more interested in the problem itself and how to solve it than in problem-solving as a means of advancing his own career.

He will also be better tempered. By doing two jobs he will free himself not only from work stress but also from much social stress. He will be under much less pressure to conform and be a regular fellow. He will be free from the extremes of economic fear. He need never feel that he has stopped growing and developing or that he has come to the end of any possibility of making progress. He will have little sense of rank, class or hierarchy in himself or in others, since his range of jobs may well cut across such artificial boundaries.

Because he will have seen more of the world and will enjoy a wider variety of experience he will be more tolerant; and because he will not feel threatened himself he will be kinder and more considerate. He will be a stimulating person to know. He will be what the most angry, bigoted, discontented and frustrated of today's workers could be if their working environment, material and psychological, were changed in the same way.

Chapter five

The relaxed society

If there are gains for the individual in a more liberal approach to patterns of work, there are also many social gains. In the last chapter some suggestions were made as to how the personality of the worker might change in a two-job system of work. The personality changes and physical benefits of the new working arrangements would in turn have a great effect on the society of which the two-job worker is a member.

It has already been suggested that the widespread introduction of part-time working and recognition of its validity must lead to changes in society's attitude towards work and leisure. Employers and workers, we have seen, would both benefit from greater flexibility in working hours and in the whole concept of work. The benefits for society as a whole would be equally far-reaching.

The new working arrangements would make possible a big and long-overdue change in society's attitude towards public service, by which is meant all the socially useful jobs which people at present do for little or no reward as a contribution to the welfare of the community or simply because it is an activity they enjoy. These jobs are at present regarded as leisure activities which we do in our spare time as a relaxation. Society's attitude towards them is full of ambiguities and inconsistencies and some of this embarrassment hinders the full mobilization of social effort when it is needed.

Let us take first of all our attitude towards elective political office, a necessary and time-consuming means of exercising democratic control over our affairs. This is usually regarded as essentially a leisure activity to be pursued in our spare time after a full day's work. Since it is impossible for most people to do a full-time job and sit in Parliament or Congress, it is conceded that those who do so must regard this as their main working activity and be paid accordingly. In local government, however, much essentially similar service on a smaller scale is still unpaid. Those elected to do such work must therefore earn their livings first and do their local government work in the evenings, at weekends and at odd times stolen from their paid jobs.

In a big local authority like the Greater London Council, where a committee chairman might need to spend half the week on council business, this is an absurdity. More than one able council committee chairman has resigned because of the time involved and has gone back to his career to make money while still in the full vigour of his powers. Many more have refused office for the same reason. At all levels of local government many of the ablest and most vigorous men and women of all parties have had to decline to serve because they cannot spare the time from a full-time job. The gaps have had to be filled by the less conscientious, by small businessmen with leisure, by the self-employed, by the retired and from the dwindling ranks of housewives without paid jobs. No party is able to field its best talent, and it sometimes shows. Decisions which vitally affect the futures of big cities and the lives of all who live in them are taken by councils composed of able people who are tired and pressed for time, and leisured folk of second-rate abilities.

One of the objections to paying people in elective office for the work they do is that this would be making politics a career, which is assumed to be undesirable. It does have the undesirable effect that a politician dependent on political rewards for a living may lose independence and become a party time-server, voting against his better judgment to safeguard his income. It is an objection that applies equally to the highest and to the lower levels of politics, and examples in Parliament and Congress show that there is something in it.

The same objection can take another form: once pay politicians and some people, less high-minded than today's voluntary councillors, will go into politics just for the money to make a career. Again examples can be quoted from the ranks of Members of Parliament and Congress, though it is fair to say that the desire to make an honest living in politics is not necessarily more ignoble than the pursuit of self-importance and status which motivates many unpaid politicians today.

A two-job economy would enable us to pay local government councillors for the work they do without incurring the objections usually made today. Those paid need not become either careerists or pensioners; they would retain their original jobs on a part-time basis and be paid for their part-time work in local government. They would have time to do the work required of them, and would have no excuse for neglecting it. Payment would not be so high as to amount to a career lure, but it would enable many to serve who would otherwise not be able to afford it. With more manageable commitments, people in politics would have time to do both their jobs properly, to the great benefit of the community.

Magistrates similarly are drawn from the relatively restricted field of those who can take time off during the day for court duties. In order to widen the field as much as possible a large body of magistrates is recruited and the duties spread among many so that nobody need assume a commitment for more than perhaps one day's duty a fortnight. Even so, the leisured, the retired and the businessmen dominate the bench to an extent out of all proportion to their numbers in the community as a whole, simply because they have more time to spare than anyone else, and the bench is therefore not fully representative of the society it serves. A paid bench of part-time lay magistrates would have the advantage of allowing its members to devote more time to this work and thus to become more experienced. But this could only be done effectively if part-time working was accepted as normal throughout all the occupations from which the magistrates are drawn.

In hospital committees, and in the other spheres in which the work of a public service is supervised by elected or appointed lay committees representing the public interest, the leisured volunteer could be replaced by the paid part-timer combining this work with another part-time job. We need not suggest that the change would be dramatic, because many voluntary committee workers do their unpaid jobs as conscientiously as if their livelihoods depended on it. Nevertheless, in such a field as the hospital service, in which people's lives and happiness may depend upon the quality of public supervision, making that supervision a paid job to which people can afford to give adequate time and thought may be expected to raise the standard. Here, too, the field of recruitment will be widened to make available the highest possible calibre of candidates for such jobs.

Making these jobs part of the paid working week, to be performed for the most part during day-time hours when people are at their most alert and least fatigued, will give many of those who serve the public in this way time for some real recreation. Instead of being cut off by their duties from contact with the ordinary people they are supposed to represent, and whose minds they are supposed to know, they will be able to take a full part in the ordinary social and recreational life of the community as well as to serve on their committees. They will have time to sit and think, to cultivate their gardens and restock their minds. Public activities will be all the better for it.

Paying for voluntary work would also make a significant contribution to the fairer sharing out of work in an underemployed society. It would in effect create a large number of new part-time paid jobs. These jobs are at present frequently done by those who already have full-time jobs. Doing voluntary jobs in their spare time makes a long, overworked day for some, while others are without any paid employment at all. The creation of this new category of paid job, and the allocation of most jobs on a part-time basis, would enable society's total work-load to be spread much more fairly.

It will be necessary to revalue leisure as an important, desirable and in a sense virtuous activity, such as it has not been acknowledged to be before. Work is an important, necessary part of human life, without which many people would find no reason for going on living. It is necessary for the individual's peace of mind and necessary for the survival of society, and has therefore always been held to be virtuous. A man at work is a man visibly doing good. Leisure, on the other hand, has always been regarded as an indulgence. Recreation is admitted to be necessary, but only in order that the human working machine can be kept in order. In an earlier age rest on Sundays was enjoined on the devout not for the purposes of sinful pleasure but so that they might reach the peak of efficiency for another six days of doing God's work. Satan found work for idle hands to do. People enjoying themselves were almost certainly doing their immortal souls no good at all, and the only morally safe form of leisure activity was to immerse oneself in a book of sermons.

We may think we have grown out of this attitude. Indeed, a religious sect originating in Japan and growing fast in the United States builds its churches in the middle of golf courses and holds that golf is an act of worship. But this has been accomplished only by substituting for leisure the concept of leisure *activity*. As long as we are not just standing there, but doing something, our souls are not in danger. Golf, as an activity, can then be elevated to the status of a nonproductive form of work and worshipped accordingly. If it is played with enough determination to take any fun out of it, it also avoids the sin of enjoyment.

Idleness, however, remains a sin for many people, and if it is combined with fun it is to be shunned as a temptation of the devil. Many people are afraid of leisure because they do not know what to do with it. This fear is surely a contributory motive impelling some people to fill every spare moment with voluntary good works. It will

59

be one of the agreeable by-products of making part-time working socially acceptable that those with a social conscience who want to serve the community in some way will be able to do so and still find time to enjoy leisure and recreation.

An important result of the mixing of jobs will be the progressive breaking down of all the social barriers—of class, status, education, race—which at present divide a community into self-contained strata. This will come about slowly but it may be the most important single benefit of the new attitude to work.

One of the main reasons for splitting the working week up between two or more jobs is to achieve variety. Much of the benefit would be lost if a worker did two precisely similar jobs. We may therefore take it that, once split-week working catches on, most of those looking for a second job will want something different from the job they are doing. Ideally, it will be not only a different activity but a job different in kind. There would be little benefit in a doctor training for and ultimately getting a second job as an accountant, another professional job of comparable status. Nor would the full benefit of change be obtained by a lorry driver who took a second job driving a taxi.

Yet once a man gets a second job that is different in kind from his first he is almost certainly getting one with a slightly different status, higher or lower. The two-job man becomes the two-status man and a breach is made in the status barrier which prevents so many people from mixing freely with their status superiors or inferiors. Of course these barriers are flexible and are already breached to some extent in leisure, politics and other voluntary activities, when people from different backgrounds have some social contact and cooperate in common aims. Yet the barriers, even today, are also surprisingly strong and durable. The lawyer and the lorry driver do not have much social contact, nor do the doctor and the dustman. They are kept apart not only by their different educational backgrounds and their class and economic status differentials, but also by the fact that there is no regular point of contact in their jobs. They do not spend time together because, except in rare cases, they have no occasion to meet in the first place. The nature of their jobs keeps them separate behind their class barriers. In some cases the class barriers are reinforced by exclusiveness based on their jobs. In institutions such as schools and hospitals, in traditionally clannish trades like mining and dock labouring, it is quite possible for a man to have few regular social contacts outside the institution or the trade in which he works. The job provides all the society he thinks he needs; it keeps him apart from the rest of society and breeds a suspicion of strangers which discourages him from seeking new contacts.

This exclusiveness and clannishness, it must be conceded, will be one of the forces working against the acceptance of a two-job system in the first place. But once the system is accepted it will begin to break down the barriers between different jobs. It could be a valuable solvent in breaking down and ultimately sweeping away the exclusive private worlds in which men work and pursue their leisure activities. It could replace them by a more open society in which social groupings are not based exclusively or mainly on jobs or the level of earnings but on personal affinities and life styles.

A man who devotes his life to one job has an incentive to mix mainly with his colleagues and his peers at the same level in other, similar firms. Many firms themselves encourage this by promoting loyalty to the business and by providing leisure and sports facilities which keep the employee on the firm's premises or among the firm's office staff after working hours. After working all day in the office, the bank clerk may then hurry off to the banks sports ground to play in the bank's cricket or tennis team against employees of another bank. This togetherness, the promise of the pleasant people you will meet and enjoy leisure with in the happy family behind the counters, figures largely in banks' recruiting advertisements. Oil companies, mines, railways, steel works, soap factories and other big concerns have gone further and built housing estates, villages and even towns to house their employees. Company towns can, it is true, equally have the effect of making employees hate the paternal firms which provide their homes and govern their lives. But even as they do so, the employees are acting as a separate, socially isolated and socially limited community.

Even when the dangers of the company town are avoided, as they usually are nowadays, a more modern social trap awaits the organization man. This is the status-club town, suburb or housing development in which all the inhabitants are self-selected as being approximately the same age, on roughly the same salary level, averaging the same number of children of the same ages, working at jobs of comparable status and at the same stage in their careers. Social life is restricted to people exactly like themselves, and the community never matures or develops, because at approximately the same point in his career each young householder finds that promotion and growing children dictate a move away to another town or a higher-status neighbourhood.

The two-job man is saved by his two jobs from these social pitfalls, with all the boredom and frustration that lie in wait. The very condition of having two jobs prevents an employee giving any one boss or company the kind of all-out loyalty which could stultify a man's intellectual, social and emotional growth, however desirable an employer might think it. This again could be one of the factors on which opposition to the two-job system might arise, exclusive company loyalty being thought in many quarters to have a cash value not to be surrendered without a struggle. But many employees know that owing loyalty to one master, on whose favour advancement depends, is a polite form of slavery. The servant of two masters is free of this particular bondage.

The way the jobs themselves are mixed could be vital in the development of a more outgoing, less compartmented society. A professional man may take a second job as a policeman because the uniform, the authority and the opportunity to cruise about the county in a patrol car appeal to some fantasy view of life that his profession does not satisfy. If he does so, he may make a new set of friends and gain a new understanding of how people think, feel and act in social circles outside his own. He also discovers what life is like without the status his professional job gives him. Many men do this, or something like it, by way of the Special Constabulary, lines, which enables them to become spare-time policemen. This has some value but the time devoted to it at present is usually not enough for the Special to become integrated into the social world of the police force. His social life as a Special is with other Specials, which is not the same thing.

There are, in fact, very many jobs of relatively low status which nevertheless could be attractive to people qualified for more remunerative jobs. The business executive who fancies the life of a taxi driver, for instance, is put off by the drop in status, the lower pay and the well-founded suspicion that if you did it long enough it would be boring and exhausting. As a part-timer retaining his business position, business status and half his business pay, however, it might be a more attractive proposition. Two-job working would have to be very firmly established in social acceptability before he would find the courage to take the part-time status and income drop for the sake of doing something that he enjoyed. But when he did so, he might find great psychological benefit. He might become less tense, more relaxed and clear-thinking in his business and much broadened in his outlook. There would also be a great gain to society. Every successful foray across the class and status boundaries would make other social adventuring easier.

Among the middle and upper classes in Britain a repressed hankering after some of the pleasures of manual work has long been apparent. The underemployed rich, in particular, have long suspected that many craft jobs must be pleasant to do and that they are missing some of the good things in life by not doing them. Some of the more strong-minded of the upper classes have actually managed to do some of the work that looked so interesting. One thinks of Sir Winston Churchill doing his bricklaying and getting an honorary union card on the strength of it. Most such would-be craftsmen would have found union opposition strong enough to prevent their taking skilled workmen's jobs, even if they acquired the necessary skill. The urge very rarely got that far. Their own sense of the fitness of things usually prevented their even attempting to sample the delights of paid work as craftsmen.

Instead, the urge has come out strongly in the thriving societies which have taken over and revived old railway lines, and in the growing popularity of industrial archaeology, which affords an opportunity to rehabilitate old steam machinery. On the railway lines run by voluntary societies retired admirals and company directors can indulge to the full an enthusiasm which is only partly a nostalgic yearning for a return to the noble age of steam and the heroic morning of the industrial revolution. It is also in part a desire to make things work, to be part of a team which is doing this and to do something constructive with one's hands. Even as a hobby, driving a steam locomotive is work. Because it involves movement and the control of 'live' steam it is easy to enjoy. But part of the enjoyment is the sense of doing something tangible, making something visibly happen which has the perceptible social benefit of transporting people. The line may be a hobby and working it self-indulgence, but the feeling is a simplified form of a very real working satisfaction which has been extracted from all too many present-day manual jobs.

Proof of this can also be seen in the activities of such a body as the Waterways Recovery Group, which organizes volunteers to give their labour in rescuing old canals from long years of neglect. In a typical venture this body of dedicated volunteers organized a working party almost a thousand strong. One rainy weekend the party gathered in one of Manchester's decaying suburbs to clean out three miles of canal which generations of Mancunians had almost filled with old iron and rubbish. Volunteers moved three thousand tons of mud-covered junk from the canal bed to help restore the canal as an amenity, and the British Waterways Board estimated their work as being worth twenty thousand pounds. There were no exciting steam engines to operate and only a few cranes and bulldozers. For most of the amateur navvies it was simply digging, hauling and moving the mud, and they worked themselves to exhaustion for two days, enjoying it enormously.

Among these weekend navvies were businessmen, civil servants, policemen, insurance agents and people from a wide variety of non-manual occupations. When allowances have been made for the enthusiasm of obsessive canal-lovers, doubtless a contributing factor, there is still clearly a deeply felt need among many white-collar workers to grapple with something more satisfyingly real and immediate than a paper problem. Weekend navvying and other voluntary labours provide some outlet for the frustrated outdoor man stuck behind an office desk.

With this example of unpaid weekend work in mind it is perhaps not too fanciful to visualize greater social benefits accruing from the provision of paid part-time manual work which a man (or woman) could do as a relief from, and contrast to, some more cerebral, more remote or less socially relevant job. There are obvious dangers. There would have to be provisions to ensure that the worthiness of a social cause was not used as a means of exploiting cheap labour to the detriment of the living standards of full-time labourers. But the application of voluntary task-force methods to social objectives on a paid, part-time basis could bring many social benefits. By providing for part-time dropping out from high-status, well-paid but boring and unsatisfying jobs, it would be possible to reduce the number of full-time drop-outs at a time when increasing numbers are opting out of the rat-race altogether. As always, the existence of the safety-valve would be a comfort and a blessing to many who would never use it. Knowing it was there would be enough.

The status mixing would be an important social benefit, just as it is in voluntary work. In a manual task force with an approved social objective the experienced manual labourer who has the strength and the know-how to do a good day's work enjoys higher status than the bank clerk who is willing but weak and unhandy. The clerk learns to respect the labourer and his labour, which he finds to be more skilled than he supposed, and the labourer learns to respect himself and his work. In time, people would become less interested in the whole idea

64

of status, essentially an expression of personal insecurity. Through a thorough mixing of people of different social status, through the experience by one individual of wide varieties of social status in the course of a week, and through the increasing realization of the irrelevance of the whole concept, status categories would wither away. As they matured in security and self-respect people once obsessed by these differentiations would stop bothering.

Work is one of the fences a man puts around himself to keep out those who might undermine his image of himself and therefore his self-confidence. If he is sexually impotent, or afraid of life, or a prey to unconquerable phobias, his job as a teacher, or lawyer, or skilled machinist, or milkman reassures him that he is a person of account to whom respect is due. The firm or institution for which he works often adopts the same image-building procedure, out of the same feelings of insecurity and lack of confidence. The image-conscious civil servant is a method actor thinking and willing himself with great intensity into the part of civil servant. He becomes part of his work; his work is not just something he does but is part of his being. There are things it is proper for a civil servant to do and he does them; things out of character for a civil servant, however personally agreeable, he does not do. He might do some voluntary work at weekends, but only if it fits the part of a civil servant relaxing from his service.

Similarly, the firm has a fixed idea of what its employees ought to be doing or not doing in their capacity as employees of this particular firm. Employees of an international oil company are discouraged from working as barmen or fish and chip shop assistants in their spare time, even though they might enjoy these jobs as entertaining diversions. The firm is insulted that employees should want more money or more interesting work than the firm itself provides. More strongly, it fears that its prestige will suffer if anyone gets to know that any of its employees are thus engaged—it could even affect share values. Where the firm or institution cannot stop it, it tries hard not to notice.

Popular acceptance of variety in employment, and in the type of employments that can be undertaken by the same person, could put an end to all such fear-ridden pomposities. It would not, of course, put an end to image-building and role-playing, since these are responses to basic human needs, but it would liberate them from the stultifying effects of identifying the man with his job and its supposed status. Members of the younger generation are already breaking away from job identification, making life more entertaining for themselves and all of us. Poets and artists have always done this. Poets have always thought of themselves as poets, who just happen to get a living by working in a bank or whatever, rather than as bank clerks who write poetry in their spare time. A painter who provides for his material needs by cleaning windows is quite sure that he is a painter, not a window-cleaner with a hobby.

Now the young workers are adopting and extending this sane and life-enhancing view of the world and their place in it. Anyone who makes a practice of picking up hitch-hikers soon discovers that the world is full of pop-singers, poets, entrepreneurs, round-the-world yachtsmen, explorers and the like, all of whom happen to need a lift. At the moment they may all be earning their livings as clerks, shop assistants or labourers but the more exciting occupations are what they are *really* doing. They may not have got far in their chosen way of life but they are working on it. And because they think themselves into the role and work on it, a surprisingly high proportion of them actually make it as poets, pop-singers and artists. In their determination to free themselves from a rigidly economic work image they are showing all of us the way to a saner, more exciting, more fulfilling and satisfying society.

The frustrations from which these imaginative ones escape find outlets otherwise in the mindless hooliganism of violence with no apparent motivation. One of the most depressing social effects of our present rigid pattern of employment is the hopelessness that it engenders. In Britain it starts low in the education system as the more likely youngsters are creamed or streamed towards those classes from which they can gain entrance to further education. On this fortunate minority, the state is prepared to pay out a total of perhaps three thousands pounds a head so that they can acquire the sort of paper qualifications which can lead to the managerial and professional jobs. On the great majority of young people who leave school at the age of sixteen, however, the state spends only the cost of some day release part-time further education of debatable value. It is supposed to make the young people better able to understand and enjoy the world they live in. It rarely qualifies them for different jobs. An attempt to give these lost ones a second chance in the Open University, while succeeding dramatically in other directions, has so far had relatively little effect on the great mass who have been schooled to expect the dull, routine jobs.

It is when the young people realize the role for which they are cast, the second-class status to which they have been assigned, that they are ready to revolt. The brighter and more energetic break out by using their wits and their imagination. But many more react against their fate by waging war on the society which has put them, and clearly intends to keep them, in dead-end jobs. The violence at football matches, the attacks on homosexuals, the mobbing of lone individuals, the gang rapes and the rest may be ascribed in part to the imprisoning effect of the repetitive jobs in which the young people find themselves, or for which they see themselves being processed. A boring and repetitive job can be interesting and relatively agreeable if it has an element of acknowledged service, if it does not go on too long, if all have to take their share, and if there are prospects of other, more genuinely interesting jobs to which the worker can expect to move. These conditions may obtain, for instance, in an Israeli kibbutz, and so the dreary jobs get done without these problems arising and without the jobs becoming intolerably repetitive. Without these conditions, protest, violence and revolt are never far beneath the surface and may erupt in strikes in the factory and violence outside it.

Chapter six

Learning something new

When a steelworks closed suddenly in Northumberland hundreds of men who had regarded themselves as aristocrats of labour, and had pay packets of appropriate size, found themselves redundant overnight. There was no skilled work in their trade anywhere near where they lived. For the older men particularly, the prospects of getting work in other steel centres—also contracting and rationalizing —were remote. Many of those without family ties drifted south in search of work.

One of these spoke of his experiences in the London area. Nobody, he found, wanted the special skill that had made him one of the highest-paid men in the North East. At the age of fifty-two he found nobody prepared to believe that his skill could be adapted to another field of work, or that he could learn another skill. After six demoralizing months looking for work he was glad to swallow a steelworker's craft pride and take a job as a school caretaker. Relating his experience, he seemed more bewildered than bitter. That the skill which had taken so many years to acquire, which had until recently been so highly esteemed and well paid, could suddenly become worthless was a serious blow to his confidence in himself as a man. The cut he was forced to take in status and self-respect was more serious even than the big drop in his standard of living. Yet he was one of the relatively lucky ones. Some of his erstwhile mates would be out of work for the rest of their lives.

Far from being an isolated tragedy, the steelworker's story is repeated many thousands of times every year in every advanced industrial country. Old skills born of long apprenticeships become useless as industries die and out-of-date processes are scrapped. The redundant middle-aged craftsman with a skill nobody wants has become a familiar figure. His age, outlook, habits of thought and previous standard of living combine to make him often an almost insoluble re-employment problem.

Increasingly today he is being joined at the employment exchange by the middle-aged manager and technician, victim of rationalization, reorganization and take-over bids. Secure jobs with prospects in well-established and prosperous firms can suddenly disappear with a change of ownership as a result of a stock exchange deal. These men too, because of their age, their specialized and narrow experience and their previous living standards, find it difficult to get new positions carrying anything like their previous pay and status. Outside the public services, almost nobody today has a completely secure job, no matter what his contract says.

The feeling of insecurity now spreading affects not only those who have already been made redundant. It gnaws at the back of the minds of many more who fear, not without reason, that it could happen to them. 'Redundancy rash' caused by this worry has already been identified by an expert on industrial diseases.[1] And in London the Secretary of State for Employment, Mr Maurice Macmillan, has warned that more and more people are going to have to change their jobs not once but several times during their working lives.[2] Training and retraining, he said, must be freely available to those who need it.

Yet for many if not most of these made redundant today retraining is little more than mockery. True, government and private industrial retraining schemes exist and are being substantially expanded. But their successes have been almost entirely with young men who are adaptable, often not yet burdened with heavy family responsibilities and have little or nothing to unlearn.

With the skilled over-forty-fives it is a different matter. They have been settled for years, have acquired responsibilities, status, ingrained working habits and prejudices. They have to face retraining at a time when they are worried, set in their ways and perhaps physically deteriorating. Worst of all, they know that even if they undergo retraining successfully they will be right at the end of the queue when an employer in their new trade is looking for labour. The risk of humiliation and disappointment at the end of it all does not make the retraining process attractive to older men or put them in the right frame of mind to pursue it successfully. For those workers who have been used to some variety of activity within their jobs, such as railwaymen, adaptation to a new job may not be too difficult. But a man who has done one rather static and repetitive job all his life, even if a skilled one, will not find it easy to overcome the age barrier and pick up a new skill. He needs not only a new skill but a new attitude to his work and to life in general. Retraining when he is fifty and out of work cannot give him this.

In the age of changing jobs the two-job man is more happily placed than most. What others regard as a major tragedy and humiliation—the need to find another job—he takes in his stride as a fact of life which he has long ago learned to accept and with which he has cheerfully come to terms. Change is part of the pattern of his working life. He expects to learn new skills and looks forward to doing so. He has no lifelong commitment to any one trade or firm. He owes no permanent loyalties. He is psychologically equipped to cope with a working world in transition, without certainties and without sentimentalities. He knows the world of work is not so cosy today as it once was for many people but he feels that it has more to offer in the course of a lifetime than used to be the case.

Most important, perhaps, Multipurpose Man does not find retraining any sort of humiliation or personal crisis. He does not wait until he is wholly unemployed and feeling insecure before embarking on the learning of a new skill. When he does tackle something new he also spends part of his time working at something he knows. He has the personal reassurance of continuing to exercise a known skill while he puts his mind to acquiring a new one.

Early in his career he may spend a few years working full time at one job, so that he masters a particular skill and also builds up a body of more generalized skills and knowledge which serve as a basis for ventures into new fields of work. After a few years he will switch to working part time at his first job and spend half his working week training for another. When this training has been completed and when he has worked in this new trade he will never be experienced in fewer than two jobs. He will never be in the position of having all his employment eggs in one basket. If he should ever find himself in the unlikely situation of losing both his current jobs at once, he will still be better placed than the plodder who has never before changed jobs. He will be doubly equipped to get a new one, having more than one skill to offer; and he will be better prepared to learn a new skill if he has to. In a society which is decreasingly likely to offer long-term job security these are advantages of some importance.

In one way, though, the two-job man would help the man with only one skill who is made redundant in middle life. For he would help to take away the stigma which at present attaches, however mistakenly, to retraining. Because retraining today is something that happens to people who have lost their jobs or who have never had skilled jobs it is rejected by many of those who need it most, the middle-aged redundant, for it is thought to bear the stamp of failure.

A man who needs retraining is thought to be a man who has failed at one job. Even though he knows his own redundancy was none of his fault, a redundant worker fears the outside world puts this construction on retraining. Having suffered a great blow to his pride already, he is peculiarly sensitive to such fancied slights.

The two-job man, retraining in his own time for his own purposes, has no truck with any such nonsense. Because he is seen to be working at a skilled job, nobody can say that he is a failure and it certainly does not occur to him that he is. He is in any case too interested in mastering a new technique even to think along such unprofitable lines. His own unselfconscious use of whatever retraining facilities happen to be available takes them out of the realm of rehabilitation, with which they are often at present confused, and gains recognition for them as respectable, high-status means by which a go-ahead man can improve his position.

The massive changeover from old jobs to new which has now started means that retraining is going to be an increasingly important part of our working lives whether or not two-job working catches on in a big way. Government and industry have accepted the need to invest huge sums in retraining schemes, if only as a hedge against the need to spend even vaster sums on unemployment pay. Retraining must certainly come on a large scale but Multipurpose Man could help to keep some of the costs down. Present retraining schemes for men changing from one industry to another usually involve a Government Training Centre financed by the taxpayer and the payment of subsistence to the trainees over a period of six months.

Multipurpose Man, training part time, need not call on the government for subsistence. Nor, in many cases, need he call on the resources of a Government Training Centre, for he is more likely to be acceptable to a firm as a trainee than is the redundant steelworker. A firm may be reluctant to take on an unemployed man for training because they will feel that when he is trained they will have undertaken some responsibility for employing him. They may be more willing to take on, for part-time training, a man already supporting himself elsewhere. They need take no responsibility for employing him after his training period, yet if he shapes up promisingly they can take him in for a trial period without committing themselves indefinitely if the experience does not turn out to be mutually satisfactory.

Many workers already doing full-time jobs, of course, train for new ones at night schools or at home by correspondence. It can be a gruelling process in which the student sacrifices nearly all his leisure. It has traditionally been the means by which a young man with ambitions who has missed earlier school opportunities can acquire the formal qualifications which open the way to a better job. It is most suitable for those occupations for which qualifications can be obtained by sitting a written examination. To these night students and home correspondence students can now be added students of the Open University. This was intended to be mainly a university of second chance for those whose formal schooling did not extend to higher education and it was originally envisaged that a high proportion of its students would be workers who for economic reasons had been unable to stay on at school. Fewer of these applied than had been hoped. In the event, a substantial proportion of the first year's intake were teachers with basic qualifications whose salary entitlement would be higher if they had degrees.

Many courses up to and including Open University level are taken for their own sakes as a leisure pursuit and not with the intention of qualifying for a new job. They can be taken at the student's own pace, can be dropped or taken up at will, may be spread over a lengthy period of years or simply left unfinished if interest wanes. The number and variety of such courses offer impressive testimony to the widespread desire of people of all ages to learn something new, but their use in the job-changing process is confined mostly to those at the younger end of the age range.

For the purpose of qualifying for a new job the night school or home study process tends to be a once-in-a-lifetime effort for a young man. The sacrifice of leisure and enjoyment and the long hours of study on top of a full day's work may be acceptable to a young man before he has full family responsibilities, and when the end in view is a decisive move from an unskilled to a qualified job with substantially greater career prospects. Once he has made the leap, any further study is likely to be only for promotion within the same occupation. A further course of study leading to the basic qualifications for a different occupation will not again involve the same leap forward in status and career propects. Instead it will be seen as a move sideways, and only in exceptional circumstances will it seem worth the effort to an older man.

Older men *can* be retrained successfully for new jobs, even the man of fifty who has done the same job all his working life. Provided a retraining course is programmed with his particular physical and psychological needs in mind, the over-forty-five can usually adapt to

72

a new job. But it is much more difficult for him if he is retraining for the first time in his life at this age. When the Industrial Training Research Unit, headed by Dr Eunice Belbin, researched older workers' attitudes to retraining they came up with a finding that strikingly contradicted conventional wisdom in industry. Workers who retrained most easily, they found, were those who had had several varied jobs in the course of their careers, rather than working steadily for one firm all their working lives. The man who has got used to retraining in his earlier, more vigorous and alert years knows that he can master a new job. He has done it before and it holds no fears for him. The older man who has never changed before lacks confidence in his ability to change, and his lack of confidence helps to make difficulties for him.

Multipurpose Man, programming change into his life from his early working years, is mentally and physically adapted to the rapidly changing world of the future. By employing two skills at once, he can change at a time of his own choosing. He discards one job and trains for another while still holding down a third. It may be objected that his lack of single-minded dedication will not carry him right to the top of any professional or commercial tree, and this may be true. But it will ensure that he is never an unemployable redundant executive or a middle-aged man dependent on an obsolete skill.

The two-job system could have advantages at the very beginning of a worker's career, at a time when he is still undergoing higher education. It could, in fact, save Britain from a threatened rundown of her higher education system. Nearly all who go through Britain's universities and polytechnics today have their fees paid and receive a subsistence grant from a local authority. With every year the number of school-leavers going on to some form of higher education rises and the cost rises with them. Faced with steeply rising costs and a government warning that higher education cannot expect to continue to be supported by the government on the same scale, an urgent search has started for ways of economizing without reducing the number of students.

Among the economy ideas so far put forward, to be greeted with no enthusiasm in academic circles, are a four-term academic year to make fuller use of staff and buildings; telescoping three-year degrees into two years; encouraging students to live at home and attend their nearest university or polytechnic; and the financing of higher education by means of repayable loans to students. There is even a proposal to use the Open University, mainly a correspondence and television organization and intended for 'second-chance' mature students, or school-leavers.

All these expedients are rejected by British academics on the grounds that they would lower standards, put too great a strain on staff and students, or would be impracticable. An expedient more practical and more likely to prove acceptable than any of these is the part-time university, in which the student works part time and studies part-time for a degree.

The concept of the student working his way through college is familiar enough in the United States. The idea appeals to the American tradition of self-help, and generations of poor boys have won a college education in this way. It can impose a strain on the students but many thousands of American graduates will testify that it is practical. The physical strain could be eliminated if the university were geared to part-time working instead of the student having to keep up with a normal university curriculum and earn his keep as well in his spare time. As in all the applications of the part-time system, it depends for success on part-time working being accepted, recognized and built into the system instead of being a rather shamefaced expedient for those whose parents or whose government are not prepared to support them.

In Britain a form of part-time higher education is to be found in the sandwich course system in which spells of work in industry are sandwiched between sessions at university or polytechnic. The spells of industrial work are related to the academic work and form part of the course of study. The object is not primarily one of economy, though there may be some saving in the more rational use of teaching and other resources. The normal academic year is sometimes abandoned altogether and the student may spend six months in college followed by six months in industry, allowing for the use of college and staff for the whole of the year instead of observing the usual vacations. The student is not expected to keep himself at college out of his earnings during his spells in industry. He gets a local authority grant for subsistence during his time in college in the normal way. Nevertheless, the principle of moving from the lectureroom to industry and back again during a course of study is accepted and established.

A part-time university would not be the same as working one's way through college in the traditional American manner, nor would it simply be a further extension of the sandwich course system. Though it would build on principles accepted in these forms of education it would be in essence something quite distinct from either. It would be based on the principle of the two-job system. Study for a degree course would be treated as a part-time occupation, not a spare-time occupation. The job with which the student occupied the rest of his time would be a normal part-time job, not necessarily related to his course of studies.

In the part-time university, courses would be rearranged so that a part-time student could take a course while working at a job elsewhere for half the week. The traditional terms and vacations would be abandoned and a new academic year instituted. The courses would take longer to complete, but probably not twice as long as the present three-year courses. There would be some time saved by spreading the course over a longer period of each year. Possibly a three-year course could be completed in four or four-and-a-half years. The staff and equipment would be more fully employed, though the staff too might be working half time. The throughput of students, assuming a part-time degree course of four-and-a-half years, would be something like one-third higher using the same staff and equipment resources. As in today's industrial sandwich course, it would be desirable to programme in each course one or more vacations of at least a month so that students could go abroad.

Not every job would be suitable for combining with a part-time degree course. Heavy manual work or very intensive work requiring a high degree of concentration might cause some strain when combined with a rigorous course of studies. A more limiting factor, particularly in the early stages of any such scheme, might be the scarcity of suitable jobs within reach of the major centres of learning, though these would increase as part-time work became more generally accepted.

It would probably not be possible for students working part time in this way to keep themselves entirely without assistance during the period of their courses. But it should be possible to reduce the amount spent on student subsistence while allowing them a higher standard of living than the present grant affords. Even if the new arrangement did no more than peg expenditure on student subsistence at its present level it would make a substantial contribution to the economy. It would make possible the preservation of higher education free from the cuts in standards and availability which threaten it at times of financial stringency.

An even greater gain would be a social one. In the part-time university students would not feel themselves to be an *élite* cut off from

75

the working class, as they sometimes do today. As part-time workers in a society in which part-time working was normal and in which most of their fellow-workers would also be part-timers, students would be fully integrated in a working society. They would be accepted and judged on their merits as workers during their working hours. In their study hours students would gain from their working lives a first-hand understanding of how the real world works. Their working contacts would serve to keep their studies in touch with reality.

The attitude of students themselves might be expected to undergo a significant change. Not being cut off as a privileged caste from the non-university worker, they would feel fewer of the doubts and uncertainties about their moral position which affect some of them and which could be contributory causes of some of the student unrest of recent years. Isolated in their academic communities, students have sometimes found the need to demonstrate their concern with the issues and problems of the world at large by importing these on to the university campus. Their concern would no doubt remain. But it would be expressed in real working situations and be subject to the discipline of a genuine struggle about real issues instead of exploding inside the university to disrupt the academic community over relatively trivial issues. It has sometimes seemed in the recent past that university authorities have had to bear the brunt of student anger and frustration caused by bodies and institutions remote from the campus and not easily accessible to students. Working students would have other outlets for their real concern in association with their workmates. University life might become more peaceful in consequence.

Working part time and studying part time for a degree might seem a harsh and exhausting way to gain a qualification. It would, in fact, be a good deal less exhausting a life than many American students have experienced in working their way through college, supporting themselves by spare-time work while taking a full-time course alongside companions lucky enough to have well-off parents. In some ways it might be a much healthier existence, subjecting the student to less mental strain even if it kept him physically more active. A student who graduates at the age of twenty-one today may have been competing in the education rat-race since the age of five. For sixteen years he will have been pushed on, coaxed over examination hurdles, threatened all the time with the loss of all he has worked for if he fails. Small wonder that by the time he gets to university many a student is ready to crack up. By the time he starts at college he is in urgent need of a break from the relentless pace of constant credit-chasing and in need, too, of a start to finding his feet as a man and a citizen. A part-time university which gave him these might well make for some harassed, over-driven students the difference between suicide and success. By taking things more slowly he would absorb knowledge more thoroughly. At the end he would be more mature as a person as well as more firmly in command of his subjects as a graduate.

Chapter seven

Winning the endgame

Nothing in a man's working life today is so unbecoming and so brutal as the manner of his leaving it. Often the process proves fatal. The harder a man has worked before retirement, the more likely he is to be cheated by death of the golden hours of leisure which were to have been his reward.

Consider the perfectly normal life-cycle of a contemporary worker, let us say a middle-ranking employee of a large commerical concern. He entered the firm at the age of twenty-two in a low-grade clerical capacity and has been with it man and boy ever since. He was not quite so unenterprising as this history suggests: on several occasions he looked round for other jobs with the idea of bettering himself and on one occasion he went so far as to secure the offer of another job. When this happened his kindly employer pointed out to him that if he left he would lose very substantial pension benefits. A small rise by way of recognizing his enterprise kept him loyal to the old firm.

Peter Plodder, if we may give him a name, was no whizz-kid. The heights of the business world were not for him. But he was honest, reasonably intelligent, loyal and biddable and he made up in diligence what he lacked in flair. He was the sort of reliable employee every firm is glad to have to make sure the company's procedures are conscientiously carried out. Over the years he rose slowly, grade by grade, to a position of some responsibility and status. There were times in his forties when he feared that office intrigue or a take-over bid might cost him his job, and he safeguarded his position in the only way he knew, by extra hard work and loyalty. When the company needed him he often worked evenings and weekends without even thinking of overtime pay.

This left him little time or energy for cultivating his own interests, but in truth he did not have any other interests. The job was his life. Most of his friends were his office colleagues. The firm's progress, its personalities and its gossip provided him with inspiration, social life and entertainment. He had a wife and children, it was true, but he saw little of them. His wife was a companion for him because he could talk about his colleagues to her and she was interested because she had met them at the firm's annual dinner. With his son and daughter he found it increasingly difficult to communicate because they had no interest in his life at work.

In his late fifties Peter Plodder began to worry about his retirement. He told anybody who asked that he was looking forward to it because it would give him a chance to give more attention to his roses. He did not in his secret heart care all that much about roses and dreaded retirement but he was a conventional person, eager to do what was expected of him, and he understood that an eagerness to cultivate roses was the proper attitude for a man approaching retirement. In his early sixties colleagues encouraged this attitude. 'You're lucky, Peter, old man,' they would cry. 'Another couple of years and you'll be able to put your feet up in your garden.' Peter Plodder heartily agreed, like the good fellow he was.

When retirement day came, the office did him proud. His colleagues presented him with gardening equipment, wished him many happy years in the enjoyment of it and asked him to think of them as he used it. There was a lunch and the presentation of a clock from the directors, and in making a modest speech of thanks Peter Plodder promised to keep in touch with his old colleagues. They sang 'For he's a jolly good fellow'.

Peter Plodder came up from his suburb to meet old colleagues twice in the first month, twice in the next three months and once in the following year. His old colleagues always professed themselves glad to see him, but he could not keep up. The gossip involved people he did not know, intrigues took new and puzzling turns and he himself had nothing to contribute. He cultivated his roses with dogged persistence but his wife noticed that he seemed a bit distracted and lost. He became morose and it was difficult not to be irritated at having him around the house all day; it meant changing her own well-established routine.

About two years after retirement Peter Plodder caught a chill and died. There were perfectly sound medical reasons but the real reason, his wife knew, was that he could not adjust to retirement. Overnight he had changed from being busy, useful and wanted, to being idle and in the way. One day he was respected, a somebody; next day he was a nobody. The psychological shock was too much for him. Conditioned to work hard for forty years, he could not adjust suddenly to a new life of idleness. Having been part of a secure society, with an assured position, he found that he no longer belonged. Bewildered and disorientated, he lost the will to live.

Not all those in Peter Plodder's position fail to adjust. Some make the necessary adjustment easily and enter happily on a new and quieter phase of their lives. A few find genuine liberation in the chance retirement brings to order their lives more in accordance with their real interests. But there are many thousands of Peter Plodders retiring every year. And if they do not all fail quite so dramatically as he, very many of them find in retirement not the happiness they had hoped for but disappointment, frustration, boredom and rapid physical and mental deterioration.

Multipurpose Man has none of these problems. He does not invest all his working life and loyalty in one firm. Leaving a firm, any firm at any time, is not a worry for him. For him there is no rigid dividing line between his active working life and the compulsory pottering of old age. There is no moment of false bonhomie when his colleagues gather round to drink his health and say, in effect: 'This is your life —and you've had it.'

He will not perhaps be working so hard at seventy as he was at fifty but as long as he has his faculties he will be involved with life. He will be an active, paid-up member of the human race. He will have a reason for living.

For the two-job man, the later stages of his life are simply a continuation of a strategy worked out many years before. Early in his working life he began to divide his interests, working part-time at one job while he learned another, changing industries and jobs whenever he felt the need of a new challenge. His life has been one of change and variety and it continues in the same way as he grows older. He is used to change. Adaptability to new work, new interests, new surroundings, new people, is one of the skills he has acquired over the years.

In two important ways he is particularly well equipped for the later stages of a varied working life. He is socially more self-sufficient than the one-job man. He enjoys company and fits well into it but he does not depend psychologically on any one social group. His friends of longest standing are not likely to be his workmates. They will more likely be people with whom he has a community of ideas and interests, a community which will endure through changes of job. He is likely to be at the same time more socially resourceful and less dependent on his social contacts than the one-job man.

He will also be less status-conscious and status-dominated. At any one time over a period of twenty or thirty years he may have had one job of higher status, one of lower. In one job he may be an acknowledged expert, in another a semi-skilled employee gaining experience. He has learnt over the years that status, or the lack of it, is part of the job, not part of the person, and is of no personal importance. If he is a skilled man holding an important post part time, that experience and attainment, and the acknowledgment that goes with it, give him a self-assurance and emotional security that carry him serenely through jobs where his personal position is less important, though the job may be rewarding in other ways. If he is not skilled enough to hold any job of great responsibility his self-confidence is supported by his experience of working on equal terms with colleagues who in the other part of their working lives hold highly responsible jobs. The dustman does not feel himself to be a low-status person when his colleague for part of the working week is a doctor. In a society where the two-jobs system is operating fully, personal status measured in terms of work hierarchy or income becomes quite meaningless and is seen to be so by all. Having no dependence on work or income status for his self-confidence, the two-job man has little or no psychological difficulty in adapting to a slower pace and declining abilities late in life. At no time does he suffer deprivation from the removing of status props to the personality.

The retirement problem of the one-job man is often that of how to fill empty days after his life's work is done. The two-job man does not have this problem. He has no single life's work and no empty days other than those he has chosen to keep free of activity. His problem is simply that of adapting his activities to fit his abilities and interests at different stages of his life. In early life he may want an active, physically demanding life. In middle life he may be more concerned to stretch his brain to meet intellectual challenges. Later on, he may want a more contemplative life with opportunities to pursue interests that have remained unexplored from busier days. Or he may want more movement, more involvement with the community, or simply more fun. Growing older affects people in different ways. For the two-job man the later years are a time for consulting his own tastes and doing what comes naturally.

Multipurpose Man will probably be moving towards his later interests in middle life, when the body may already be demanding an easing of the strains of early endeavour. The man whose idea of the perfect job for his declining years is keeping a country pub or a village shop will probably have started it on a part-time basis in his fifties, as a relaxation from more strenuous affairs. When the time comes to give up double-job working for a single part-time job he will know whether pub-keeping or village shopkeeping is really what he wants to do. If it is not, he will have had time to explore something else. Almost certainly, he will be doing *something*, as long as he has his health and strength, though what he does will no longer be limited by the primary need to earn a living. Pensionable age will become a movable feast but it will bring with it opportunities to serve the community by doing voluntary work, to work at some personal project or pursue some personal interest. As has been suggested, much more voluntary work will be paid on a part-time basis than is the case now, so that a man may earn enough for his needs without making a career job of it. Older people will be in demand as secretaries of amenity societies, book-keepers for charities and for all the jobs that help local communities to function. Their personal projects might be long-cherished small business ventures, the compiling of local histories, painting or plant-collecting. Interests could include a wide range of leisure and sporting activities. The two-job man is likely to treat his later jobs as an opportunity to have fun and gain some interests. He will attack his leisure activities with the systematic application he might give to a new part-time job. The adaptability, the curiosity and the self-starting ability he has cultivated all his life should ensure that in his sixties and seventies, as much as in his thirties and forties, he is never idle and never bored.

Much of what has been said about the two-job man's adaptability to approaching age is of course a description of what an intelligent, fortunate minority are already contriving to do today. It is a commonplace that a man ought to plan in middle life for his later years, that he should find something to do after he retires and that he should escape the isolation of retirement by involving himself in community or local leisure affairs. The well-adjusted folk who take this admirable advice offer ample proof, in their active, cheerful lives, of its wisdom. But for every one who survives the shooting-Niagara-Falls experience of retirement and bobs up triumphantly in the pool below there are many more who sink without trace. For many men retirement, and for many wives the death of a husband, marks the effective end of life as a social human being. Lack of personal resource, psychological shock, loss of social confidence or, more simply and more crushingly, a sudden drop into poverty, to all intents and purposes removes them from the land of the living.

What is at present possible for the lucky few ought to be possible for all. This is not the case today. The lucky few who have eased their way into later years without a formal break at sixty-five have been intelligent enough to seize opportunities when they occurred. But this is not to say that those who fail to achieve this easier transition are unintelligent. On the contrary, relatively few are today in a position in which they can choose to change their work patterns by stages as age approaches, instead of making a dramatic break on reaching official retiring age.

Those who can choose are only able to do so because the great majority are forced by the circumstances of their jobs to soldier on until they can claim their pensions. Early preparations might entail dropping out of highly competitive employment and perhaps moving to a country town, buying or starting a small business or taking up one of the decreasing number of jobs with a craft content. It is no doubt open to any individual to make the necessary moves in time, or to start earlier to acquire some capital and some new skill if these are required. But as things stand at the moment, society can only survive if this remains the option of a small minority. The few who drop out of the rat-race depend for their well-being on the great majority staying in it.

Good luck to the ones who get away to become boat-builders or village publicans, but they can only do so successfully if a vast, disciplined army of their fellow-citizens remain at steady jobs providing all of us, including the getaways, with food, transport, health services and much else. The fact that today a minority are able to organize their working lives in a way that gives personal satisfactions free from major stress does not mean that the problem has been solved for the majority any more that the existence of the big houses of the rich means that homelessness has been eliminated.

A society in which multiple part-time working had increased the work mobility of every citizen would make possible for all the easing of the aging process which is now available only to the lucky few.

Every retirement problem is different. It depends very much on the personality, the interests, the skill, the financial resources and the health of the individual. Many people will want to take up a new activity as they grow too old for the more strenuous pursuits. Others will be absorbed in what they are already doing and want nothing better than to be allowed to go on doing it, simply reducing their physical commitment as age takes its toll. There are men who approach retirement impatiently, only waiting to earn their pension

83

before moving, with plenty of energy in hand, to what really attracts them, perhaps to an interesting but ill-paid job now acceptable without too great a loss of living standards when supported by a pension.

A multi-job society would make it easier for all men and women approaching their senior years to make whatever job arrangements suited them best. In particular it would ensure that nobody other than by choice would need to pass from full employment to idleness overnight, and nobody would need to be quite without an occupation.

Today's over-rigid retirement pattern depends to some extent on today's pensions system, under which a person must reach a particular age, often in the same job, to earn a pension big enough to live on. Once retired at sixty-five a man can earn only a few pounds a week if he is not to lose most or all of his state pension, even though he has contributed to it all his life. These financial restraints impose a fixed pattern of retirement which condemns many over-sixty-fives to unnecessary and unwanted idleness. Like the work pattern, the pensions system would have to become more flexible in harmony with it. This would need new government thinking and new legislation but there is nothing inherently difficult about making the necessary changes.

As technology takes over more and more routine jobs unemployment is becoming an increasing problem in many industries. In mining, transport, steel and many other industries this is not a temporary recession but a permanent reduction of the labour force is needed, in the case of coal-mining possibly the phasing out of a whole industry. It is understandable that in these industries voices should be raised demanding earlier retirement as a means of solving the redundancy problems such shrinking or dying industries create. Early retirement is also seen by some trade unionists and others as a means of reducing unemployment generally throughout the country. There have been calls to put the retirement age forward to the age of sixty or even fifty-five or, alternatively, to cut working hours dramatically all round to achieve the same ends. Many industries subject to sudden booms and recessions fluctuate between overtime and short time as the volume of orders demands. Temporary short-time working has been accepted in many cases as a fairer alternative to laying men off in a recession.

Clearly there is a case for the more equitable distribution of work. It is neither social justice nor economic sense to pay some men at a higher rate for working more than a normal working week while other men are paid a dole for doing nothing. There is a case also for substantially shorter working hours and early retirement, particularly in industries going through a period of contraction.

But while these measures have certain merits of their own they are not solutions to the problem of unemployment. They are, at best, temporary substitutes for the real solution to a major unemployment problem, which is to create new employment by establishing new industries and new services.

Early retirement does not solve an employment problem. It simply means that the middle-aged and elderly are unemployed instead of the young. There may be social arguments in favour of discriminating against the older person in this way but a man who is compulsorily retired at fifty-five is just as unemployed as the man who is sacked at fifty-five, though the former may be financially better off.

What is the man who is retired at fifty-five supposed to do? There may be some with sufficient personal resources to occupy themselves entirely at hobbies or personal projects for the next twenty or thirty years. But most men and women need an occupation at fifty-five, sixty and usually at sixty-five, as much as they did at thirty. With improved health standards most will feel fully fit and capable of work and will be anxious to have something to do. They may well be glad to get away from a boring and frustrating job, but then they would have been glad to do that at almost any time.

What they are usually not prepared to do is spend the rest of their lives 'enjoying leisure', partly because leisure may be something they do not enjoy and do not know how to handle, and partly because there is in most men and women an innate need to feel useful, to be a contributing member of society and to be a recipient of the social esteem which is the entitlement of anybody who is doing something socially useful. Many people like work, though they may dislike a particular job. They get depressed and physically ill if they are denied it over a long period. For these people, perhaps a majority of working people, early retirement is certainly no good turn in itself. It is simply an enforced and unwelcome retreat from life.

Unaccompanied by any other measure, early retirement would merely bring forward the psychological shock, the frustration, the drop in status, living standards and social esteem, and probably the depression and loss of morale which are so often brought about by retirement at sixty-five. The depression and loss of morale might well be all the greater because retirement would come at a time when the man felt that he still had many more years of active life in him.

Early retirement in a situation where other jobs were available would be another matter. Given the availability of other work, it might well be a positive step towards breaking down the restrictive pattern of work as a lifelong commitment to one industry. In this respect it might be even better if retirement came at fifty or forty-five, as it can in the armed forces.

If early retirement is seen in this light, however, it is soon apparent that it is then a step in the direction of a flexible multi-job pattern of work. For if early retirement is used as a means of inducing job mobility in middle life, then multiple part-time working can be seen as a more effective means of inducing the same end while at the same time making the transition much easier and more agreeable for the worker. For a fully flexible part-time system, in which a man changes jobs perhaps half a dozen times in a working life without ever being unemployed, allows the worker to make a change when it suits him, not at some arbitrary time laid down in advance which may not be the right psychological moment for the individual.

Under the two-job system, in fact, early retirement becomes unnecessary and irrelevant because retirement itself in its present form becomes an irrelevant conception. The worker may 'retire' from four or five jobs at different times, always keeping on another one until he feels the need to reduce his commitments to perhaps one part-time job or drop formal work altogether. But he will do it all in his own time, to be decided by himself. There will no doubt be cases in which the worker wants to stay on when he is no longer physically or mentally up to the job. Rigid retirement rules have their uses in cases where nobody would otherwise have the temerity to suggest to a dominant figure that it was time he went. But these cases would be discussed personally with the individual and he could be helped to make a change.

The elimination of formal retirement by the multi-job process would have the additional advantage of improving the status of what is now the man of retired age. It would do this in the general sense that rank and income status, in which the retired man cannot compete, would become much less regarded and in time be seen to be meaningless. But it would also raise his status by raising the status of all part-time work. In most jobs today the part-time worker is considered inferior to the full-time worker. Jobs using a high proportion of part-timers have lower status than similar jobs manned by full-time workers. Retired people eking out pensions with part-time jobs inevitably suffer this loss of status. They are usually relegated to low-grade jobs anyway, because it is the exceptionally ill-paid jobs which welcome pensioners who can subsidize themselves from their pensions. These already low-grade jobs are diminished in social status still more by being part-time jobs. To an elderly man who has enjoyed responsibility, social esteem and an assured position in the past, this may assume more importance and be more difficult to come to terms with than it would be for a younger man.

When nearly every worker is working at one or more part-time jobs as his main source of income, the present stigma attached to part-time working will disappear and the elderly worker's morale and sense of personal dignity should improve accordingly.

Part-time working will enable the elderly, within their physical capacities and inclinations, to do if they wish the jobs they may need to structure their lives and keep them in mental and physical shape to enjoy their leisure.

Chapter eight

The liberation of women

One of the fundamental human rights which women have found hardest to win is the right to a decent job. By this is meant the right to follow an occupation for which she has talent and training and in which she herself is interested and personally involved. Women have always had the right to drudgery, the right to work an eighteen-hour day as wives, mothers and maids-of-all-work. And they established very early the right to do back-breaking labour on farms or over a sewing-machine. What they have found much more difficult to win is the right to do a job which helps to fulfil a personal need for self-expression and achievement and which satisfies the urge to play a creative part in the life of the community.

Even now, when women appear to have won the battle for the right to a career, victory is conceded in a grudging spirit and is very far from complete. The employment disabilities from which women suffer still make it extremely difficult for them to compete with men for the more rewarding jobs or to advance according to their talents in their careers. It is true that they may now be doctors, teachers, engineers, scientists or business executives and work at many skilled jobs once the preserve of men. But even today their numbers in the top jobs bear no relation to their total numbers or their talent in the industry or profession concerned. There are still many fields in which they have made only a token entry and many which they have scarcely entered at all. For the great majority of women, their main opportunities for employment still lie in what has long been considered women's work: in repetitive factory work, in catering and in all the personal service jobs, ranging from nursing and serving in shops to office cleaning, which are thought particularly suitable to women's talents and temperaments.

To follow a profession, to have a career in a skilled and challenging job, a woman must make sacrifices which are not demanded of a man. Sometimes she has to sacrifice her womanhood. If she wants a career in a man's world, then she must give up ideas of marriage, or even of femininity, and behave as much like a man as possible. Those who succeed in getting to the top in such conditions may eventually emerge as formidable battle-axes with womanly attributes sternly repressed.

Or the implied bargain may be that a woman can have her career, competing equally with men, just so long as she retires to the domestic hearth as soon as the first child comes along. When the family is founded and the children are at school, she may be allowed to resume her career, ten years behind her contemporaries. If you can't keep a good woman down, this should prevent her getting to the top.

It is sometimes possible for a woman to keep her job, provided she is prepared to do nearly all the work of running the house in her leisure-time, when her male working colleagues are taking their ease and being ministered to by their wives. The man does a day's work and is then considered to have earned his leisure. The woman does a day's work and is then considered to have earned the right to cook and serve a meal, wash up and put the children to bed. If she wants the luxury of a full-time job, in today's circumstances, she is often forced to take on in addition what is more than a half-time job, the work of running the home.

If it applied only to women, part-time working would not in itself be the cure for these disabilities. A married woman may feel that a full-time job together with the work of running the home is more than she can manage; and she may then decide to reduce her commitments to manageable proportions by working part-time at a paid job and part-time as a housewife. If she does that under present circumstances she may quite well find that she cannot simply reduce her hours and go on working at the same job. If she is a business executive or a higher civil servant she will probably find that there is no provision for her job to be done on a part-time basis. If she is a teacher she may find that it is certainly possible to go on teaching, but no longer as an established member of the staff. If she is able to work within her existing profession or skilled occupation at all, it will now be as a casual with lower status, poor financial rewards and no career prospects.

Much more likely, she will find that if she wants to work part-time she will have to leave the well-paid job in which she works on equal terms with men and take a lower-paid job in her profession or a job of much lower skill and status in which her fellow-workers are all women part-timers.

Faced with this situation, the women who need the money badly will stay on in their full-time jobs and resign themselves to doing without adequate rest and leisure. Those who do not need the money so badly, but are working because they are interested in the job and get satisfaction from doing it well, are more likely to give up paid work altogether. They will feel that the full-time job puts too great a burden on them but will see no point in working part-time at some other, unsatisfying job just for extra money they do not desperately need.

In this way, for lack of the machinery to meet their working needs, many thousands of highly intelligent, expensively trained women whose skills could be contributing to their country's prosperity are lost to the professions, business and industry and turned into frustrated, complaining 'graduate wives'. Winning better education and providing more job opportunities for women simply adds to the number who experience this frustration when they marry and start families.

To the frustrations of those who have started out in worthwhile jobs, only to be defeated by the demands of the home, must be added the many more women, even today, who see the baby barrier looming ahead and do not feel that it is worth the effort to start a career in a satisfying and challenging job. They go instead for the time-filling, non-involving jobs which demand no great personal commitment and consequently can be left for home life without regret when the time comes.

There are, of course, always a few individuals who will overcome any barrier to get where they are going. It is always possible to point to a few women who manage to gain and hold down high-powered jobs as doctors or company directors, housekeep for a husband and four children and still find time for politics or charitable fund-raising. They are marvellous women and they are quite exceptional. They do not prove that the barriers are down; they show only that women of exceptional stamina, organizing power and talent can overcome the difficulties. And sometimes, even then, only when married to wealthy husbands. For most women the barriers are real and forbidding, and for many they prove insurmountable.

When a woman is determined to continue with her career and have a family, her success will perhaps still involve heavy sacrifices. Some career wives will be only too thankful to hand over the running of the home to a housekeeper and the raising of her children to nannies and boarding schools. But many will regret the delegation of their role as wife and mother to others. They will feel a real sense of deprivation

90

at seeing their children so rarely, at playing so small a part in forming their characters and at missing so many of the rewarding moments of parenthood.

Most of these difficulties could disappear if part-time working were accepted as normal not only for wives and mothers with home commitments but for everybody, man or woman, who found it convenient. Only if part-time working became the common form for jobs from the lowest level to the highest would women really be free to work on equal terms with men in any particular job. There would then be no incentive for a firm to prefer a man to a woman on the grounds that the man would be more committed. There would be no career time-lag during which the men would get ahead while the women retired for several years to start families. And there would be no excuse for designating some of the low-status jobs 'women's work' on the grounds that they were particularly suitable for workers employed on a part-time basis or for a relatively short period.

Part-time working for all, in fact, would set women free in the employment field by striking at the very basis of male superiority. In spite of all the efforts of women's liberation campaigners, it is still true today that in most families it is the husband who has the career while the wife, if she works at all, does so in a subsidiary role as far as the family is concerned. In a few families both husband and wife have careers of equal status but this is rare enough to be studied by sociologists as a phenomenon. The difficulties involved are great and a number of conditions have to be met: the two jobs must be relatively stable without frequent promotions to different locations, they must both be paid well enough to allow help to be hired for the housework and the children, and so on.

When the wife has a more important job than the husband the difficulties are even greater because the husband has to accept a deviation from the still strong social convention that the husband should be the main breadwinner. Although the wife's career is accepted in theory in many families, in practice it is usually the husband's career that comes first when there is a conflict of interest. When the husband is offered a substantial promotion if he moves to another town, it is often the wife who gives up her own career and makes a disadvantageous change in order that the husband can take advantage of his career opportunity. When the wife is offered an advantageous posting to another town she usually refuses it unless it can be shown not to affect her husband's career adversely.

Part-time working for all eases both the psychological and the practical problems involved in two-career families and puts the wife for the first time in a genuinely equal position. When almost everybody is working part-time the wife can give to her own job the same dedication that the husband gives to his. In neither case will it be a full-time life commitment. The concept of the breadwinner and the home-maker as roles for the husband and wife will no longer have social significance because wives will be offering their skills and talents on the labour market on exactly the same terms as their husbands. At the same time, there will be nothing to stop the husband assuming more of a home-making role if that is what the family wants. Until now, the wife has either had to run the home in addition to working or she has had to organize and supervise the domestic arrangements when the house is to be run by paid staff.

An American correspondent, a keen women's lib. supporter, commenting on the possibilities of part-time working, seized on this. 'Why not let the husband and wife both hold part-time jobs and devote the remaining time to family, church, hobbies, or whatever suits them?' she asked. The same thought has occurred to similar groups in Britain. So far the practical and social difficulties have been great, but if part-time work were normal and readily available any family that wanted to could organize itself in this way. Among young couples especially, the psychological barriers are already down. Many young husbands genuinely want to take a share in running the home and bringing up the children. Part-time working provides a practical way of making this possible and enabling couples to spend more time together.

These new attitudes would become possible because part-time working would take much of the competitive strain out of all jobs. For one thing, nobody's personal standing would be wrapped up entirely in one job. Many people today are identified by the world, and identify themselves, exclusively in terms of what they do for a living. Bank manager, teacher, policeman, scientist, salesman and civil servant often carry over into their private lives the attitudes, authority and status associated with their employment. Part-time working, by encouraging them to understand the feelings and aspirations of other groups of workers, would help them to broaden their outlooks, to the point where they would accept women as workers with equal rights to respect and consideration.

Themselves liberated from the demands of status-seeking and competition, men would at last be able to take the normal human interest in their wives, homes and families which they had previously
92

neglected under the pressure of getting ahead and beating their neighbours in the race to material success. They would have the time to satisfy this interest by taking a genuine, unforced share of domestic responsibilities. By doing this, and by acknowledging the equal status of their partners as co-breadwinners and domestic managers, husbands would adopt in time the attitudes necessary to make a reality of the liberation of women from enforced domesticity.

Women would be able to get out of the home and exercise the right to work without adopting the present-day attitudes of men towards their jobs. Instead of being forced to approach jobs on an all-or-nothing basis, they could view work for what it is: a necessary part of the full human experience, without which life lacks a dimension, but by no means the whole or necessarily the main interest in life. Instead of standing too close to the job, women would be able to look at it coolly and objectively and perhaps be in a better position to see where improvements could be made.

Not every woman wants to abandon domesticity. Feminists may argue that if a woman prefers home life it is because she has been conditioned to do so by generations of male domination. Whether or not that is so, for many women the preference for domestic interests is real. There will probably always be some women for whom husband, home and children offer all the activity that is needed. These would still be able to follow peaceful domestic lives but their number might be expected to diminish if outside jobs were made more readily available on a part-time basis and if the nature of work changed perceptibly.

Part-time work for women would not be just full-time work divided by two. It would be a different kind of work from what has hitherto been available, with much greater career opportunities. With so many jobs shared between two people, there would be fewer office empires and a much less egotistical approach to work. There would necessarily be more consultation and cooperation instead of giving orders. In many cases a more relaxed working environment has been created by enlightened managements on the advice of industrial psychologists as a means of getting better productivity. The requirements of part-time working would extend and reinforce this trend and have a civilizing effect on employment conditions generally. In this way, too, offices and factories would become much less exclusively masculine in their ruling atmosphere, more places in which women could positively enjoy working. Part-time employment would create at work more of the family atmosphere that the better employers are already trying to achieve. Such an atmosphere would be congenial to many women who are repelled by the hierarchies and formal disciplines of office and factory and prefer domestic life.

If women are sometimes repelled by the conditions, the atmosphere and the inferior position in which employment puts them, men sometimes have very real reasons for hostility to the employment of women. In many cases women have been prepared to accept lower pay than men because they did not need the money so badly. Girls worked only to fill in time before marriage, often living cheaply with their parents. Married women worked to add some extras to the family standard of living, already basically provided by the male breadwinner. In fields of employment where men and women were doing the same or comparable work, this pin-money approach to pay made effective trade unionism much more difficult to organize and helped to keep wage levels of both men and women depressed.

For years this economic weakness helped to create and maintain prejudice and strengthen the hands of those who wanted 'men's work' and 'women's work' kept in separate compartments. Though equal pay for men and women doing similar work is now an accepted principle, embodied in the law, it is still possible to discriminate against women by employing only women on some lower-paid jobs. Even where the principle of equal pay has been accepted by employers, the prejudices of the old days linger on, as when bus drivers refused to accept women colleagues behind the wheel. They feared that this would weaken their wage-bargaining position.

Though it is still strong in places, the old prejudice is dying. It could be finally laid to rest by a new pattern of employment in which everybody, men and women, worked part-time at different jobs as a matter of course. There would be a greater tolerance for all colleagues and workmates; no worker would be as closely identified with his work as he is now and so no worker would be as concerned as some are today about the effect on the status of the job of the employment of different groups or individuals. Workers would be more used to mixing. There would be a breakdown of the old prejudice against women because the old economic argument would finally fail. By having alternative employment on which to fall back while pressing demands for higher pay, trade unionists would be in a strong bargaining position. Since the great majority of women workers would be no pin-money girls but serious breadwinners on equal terms with their husbands, they would have as strong motivation as their husbands to protect and improve their pay and conditions.

Instead of acting as if they were two different species, with different and sometimes conflicting economic aims, men and women workers would be able to work together as fellow human beings sharing aspirations and attitudes as well as work. Just as men and women would find a common interest in their home life, so they would find a common interest in their working life. Both male and female attitudes would tend to die out and both men and women would build up a common attitude as work-people or employees. This would be a true liberation of the woman.

For the great majority of industries, the change brought about by the part-time pattern would be substantial. Even where women are in theory employed on equal terms with men, they are in practice usually a minority in a men's world, their numbers decreasing in the upper ranks. By cutting the hours of work for all in a particular company, by eliminating the need for a competitive rat-race and diminishing the rewards to be gained from it, and by relaxing the whole atmosphere, conditions would be created in which there would be no domination of one sex by the other. In factories and offices women would be neither slaves nor pets.

After centuries of being at a disadvantage because of their domestic interests, they would start the new era on equal material terms but with a decided psychological advantage. Because of their multiple role as mothers, housekeepers, wives and workers in the past, they have long been used to dividing their attention among a number of different activities. Multipurpose Woman has been a reality for many years, sometimes exercising in the course of twenty-four hours the skills of a cook, a housekeeper, a children's nurse, a child psychologist, a buyer, a decorator and a manager, quite apart from whatever paid part-time work she might have been doing. Switching rapidly from job to job, and from problem to problem, turning her hand to whatever needs doing and keeping several activities on the go at once have long been part of what it takes to be a woman. What has sometimes been despised as an inability to concentrate on a single sustained effort has in fact been a mental and psychological agility without which the average wife simply could not get through a busy and varied day.

Far from having what men, with false superiority, have dubbed a lack of staying power, women can fairly claim that it is they who embody the higher human achievement in their quick-change adaptability, while men suffer the disability of one-track minds which can only work efficiently if applied to one matter over an

95

extended period. If a change is as good as a rest, then it is the woman's ability to switch smoothly from subject to subject, and from task to task, picking up the threads instantly, which represents the most productive use of human resource. She can keep going efficiently long after a man's concentration has suffered from the boredom and fatigue of spending too long on one job and his performance has deteriorated to a marked extent.

In this respect, as in many others, what difference there is between men and women is not innate but represents simply an adjustment over generations to the different roles society has allocated to them. By no means all women are well adjusted to a variety of functions, just as by no means all men are incapable of adapting rapidly from task to task. Even when the roles of men and women were more rigidly defined than they are today many did not fit easily into the roles their sex had assigned to them. In a change-over to a part-time working system women would have an initial advantage because they have been trained by their roles as women to be adaptable and to reach the peak of their abilities by working in relatively short bursts. But once the part-time plan had become the accepted norm for men and women, this difference in adaptability between the sexes would disappear. Men would learn in time to become as adaptable as women and the efficiency of the whole work force would improve accordingly.

The system of part-time working which is suggested here is quite different from most of the part-time work at present available to women. It is possible in many districts for women who want it to obtain part-time work in factories, offices, hospitals, shops or catering establishments. Part-time work for women as cleaners, domestic workers and in other low-grade capacities is certainly no novelty. Part-time work for teachers and doctors also exists, though it is harder to find. But very little of this represents a liberation for the woman. Far from setting her free, all too often it is simply an extension of her position as family drudge. In addition to all her duties at home, she is working to add to the family income.

Apart from the money it brings in, it is sometimes welcome as a means of escaping briefly from domestic responsibilities and getting a bit of extra interest. Many women who go out cleaning do it much more for the sake of the company and the chance of a gossip. The pay may be poor in cash but it is sometimes an implicit part of the contract that part of the emolument takes the form of gossip. When two housewives pay the same cash rate for domestic help, the one who is willing to gossip about her family's life and problems gets more willing service and is likely to keep her help longer.

This sort of part-time work may be welcome for the amelioration it brings to the lot of the housebound wife, or the underemployed and life-starved prisoner in the suburbs. But it is in no sense any real liberation. The prisoner is let out on licence from time to time but she is let out in strictly controlled conditions for a period of association. Her basic conditions of domestic servitude remain unchanged.

Universal part-timing would be a real liberation for all women, and especially for wives and mothers, because it is a real levelling-up process. The right to a satisfying job is recognized as being equally valid for men and women and both sexes are enabled to exercise this right. For such a work-pattern to come into effect at all there has to be a transformation in society's whole approach to work and this involves a radical re-appraisal of women's right to work. The system can only work successfully if all women, whether single or married, with or without children, are accepted equally with men as being part of a single, integrated national body of workers, all of whom have the right to order their working lives in the way that suits them best as individuals. A demand for full-time commitment automatically excludes those for whom such a commitment is impossible. It leads to a situation in which full-timers, mostly male, hold all the most satisfying and best-paid jobs while most of the part-time jobs are means of exploiting underpaid women.

When most of the top jobs are held by part-timers, however, it is a fair bet that more than half of these will be women.

Chapter nine

A new way to use time

The use of leisure, we are frequently told, is now or will shortly become one of the major problems of the age of affluence. As the working week gets shorter, how are we to occupy the endless idle hours? Are we equipped by education, training or habits of mind to meet the personal challenge leisure presents to us? Is there not now an urgent need to re-educate and re-train so that when our leisure hours lengthen beyond our capacity to fill them with drinking, do-it-yourself carpentry and fishing we shall have further resources to throw into the breach?

To some extent the problem is a false one, or at any rate it has been falsely stated. There is a leisure problem, though it is not the one usually presented to us. There is also a work problem. Both are really facets of the same overall problem, which is how we are to use our time.

A busy executive and a factory worker have the same leisure problem: how to find the time and energy after a long, tiring day to come to life as human beings and live their own lives. They have very little spare time in which to be themselves and not enough energy left at the end of the day to be sociable, mentally or physically active or creative.

When their hours of work are drastically reduced, both men have a different leisure problem: how to fill the time that was previously occupied by work. They are now free to do all the things they always thought they wanted to do. After a period of adjustment they take to golf and cocktail parties or fishing and allotment digging, according to fancy, and are then considered to have solved the leisure problem. In fact, they may have done nothing of the kind. They may now be spending part of their time doing things which bore them instead of things which merely exhaust them. They may be following their respective leisure pursuits not because these are the activities that have always fascinated them but simply because social conventions suggest that they are suitable ways for executives or factory workers to spend their non-working hours.

If they lose their jobs altogether, both men have a great increase in leisure. Indeed, all the time they previously spent working is now leisure time, or 'playing' as it is called with grim humour in Lancashire. Yet they are then not said to have a leisure problem, but a work problem. They have this problem even when investment or a pension gives them an assured income so that the earning of money is not of vital importance for material survival. They have a work problem not only because there is in most men a practical need to earn a living. There is also a psychological need to be a contributing member of society, doing something to earn the respect of other people, and a need to be doing something which maintains self-respect.

The present-day problem of work or leisure is accentuated by the very uneven spread of both among the population of most advanced industrial countries. Despite the trend to shorter working hours, some workers at all levels from labourer to managing director are working sixty hours a week or more, with virtually no usable leisure time, while others are totally unemployed. What all of them share is a problem of how to organize a pleasant and acceptable division of their time among a number of activities, so as to achieve a viable, balanced and enjoyable life free from undue physical or psychological stress.

For the unemployed man without a private income, finding a job that will provide a living is the first essential. For most other people the problem is either finding time for other activities after the day's work or finding other activities to occupy available time. In neither case is it necessarily a help in finding a solution to label activities 'work' or 'leisure' according to whether payment is made for doing them. This is especially true when the decision to pay or not to pay is based almost entirely on commercial rather than on social values.

A factory worker who plays the drums in a dance band during the evenings and at week-ends is thought of as a working man with a moonlighting job, even though he finds his band work enjoyable and a relaxation from his factory work. If the same factory worker should find relaxation in playing chess or acting as honorary secretary of the local gardening society he becomes a working man with a leisure interest. He is regarded in this light even if he finds being an honorary secretary much more like 'work' than playing in a band. A professional footballer is a man with a job, because he is paid to do it, whereas a man with a pension or private means who spends forty hours a week as unpaid chairman of a city council committee is unemployed. An unpaid marriage guidance counsellor is taking part in a leisure activity whereas a paid marriage guidance counsellor has a profession. One man's work is another man's leisure activity.

It may therefore be as well to leave aside any preconceptions of what is work and what is leisure and consider what a man might regard as a stimulating, healthy and well-balanced use of his time. The formula will clearly vary from person to person but it is possible to list some of the kinds of activity most people would like to include in a happy life. Almost all the activities can be enjoyable in themselves but can also cause stress if carried on to excess or if too much has to be attempted in too little time.

The first requirement is a job, that is to say an activity which requires the regular and sustained exercise of a faculty for some social end and which earns self-respect and the respect of others. For most people, though not for all, it needs to earn money as well. A job as defined here may be of any duration from a few hours a week to practically every waking moment. But to fulfil the need for social respect it needs to be done with a certain amount of regularity and to engage a significant proportion of a person's time. There is no necessary reason why it should be commercial or why any person should confine himself to only one such activity.

The second requirement is recreation for mind and body. Under this heading come all forms of exercise, outdoor and indoor games, hobbies, studies, reading, entertainment and pleasures of most kinds. Indeed, almost any change of activity can be some kind of recreation. Laying bricks can be a recreation if you have spent the day studying documents. Studying documents as an official of a trade union or local society can be a recreation for a bricklayer. As Marie Lloyd used to sing, a little of what you fancy does you good, and whatever a person enjoys can be recreation.

Most people feel the need to devote part of their time to social activity, in which they meet other people and become participating members of a group. For some the family may be human society enough but most people need to establish and maintain contacts with a larger social grouping. Parties, drinking, visiting, voluntary work, community activity and most forms of recreation help people to fill this need.

In any ideal distribution of time many people would include some time devoted to a personal interest or pursuit. Not everybody finds that his job, his recreation or his social life gives him a personal interest in which he feels deeply concerned as an individual; and if other activities do not give this he may want one that does. Of course, in one sense family life provides such a personal commitment. A man or woman with a family and children has a personal home life with claims quite distinct from work, recreation or social activity, even though part of that personal life may be spent in recreation or social activity. For some men and women the family and the home provide all the personal interest they feel their lives need. But there are some, even though happily married and devoted to their spouses and their children, who still feel the need to spend some time pursuing a personal interest which is more than a recreation. The English housewife who saved up for a trip on the Trans-Siberian Railway because it was something she had always wanted to do was an example of this kind of personal interest. It was not recreation in the ordinary sense, nor yet social activity. The long-distance single-handed sailor might be another example.

Self-development in the sense of learning or studying might be another essential claimant for some people's time. For such people a healthy, well-balanced life must include some activity in which they can feel that they are developing and changing themselves for the better. A course of study for a new qualification is the most obvious example but a body-building routine or the starting of a new small business might have the same motivation.

All these kinds of activity are important in varying degrees in most people's lives. They are not sealed compartments, mutually exclusive. Voluntary work, to which many people devote a significant proportion of their time, may to some people be recreation, to others social activity and to a further group a job. Watching TV may be recreation, a social activity or a personal interest. Specific activities will constitute different elements of the life pattern for different people. It is even possible for a few people to find in one job the elements of work, recreation, social activity, personal interest and self-development. But most people find these necessary elements, when they do find them, in a variety of activities.

Present rigidities of work make it difficult to fit in all these elements. A man with a satisfying, responsible job may have to devote so much time to it that he has little time left for recreation, or for his personal home life, and none at all for social activity or self-development. Many people are only able to pursue a cherished personal interest if they cut recreation and social activity to a minimum. One result is that the people who work hardest, under the most intense pressure, are the ones least likely to attain the properly balanced mixture of activities which would enable them to stand up to those pressures successfully. We frequently hear of politicians who have little time to spend with their wives: one prominent American politician had to resign his post as a key presidential aide because his wife threatened to divorce him if he did not spend more time at home. More often in such situations the couple quietly split up. The more successful a man is, the heavier is the pressure on him to devote more and more time to his work.

Achieving a satisfactory balance of activities is made more difficult by the arbitrary division of work and recreation into paid and unpaid activities. If a man's job is a paid one he may have to spend on it more time than is healthy because he needs the overtime payments to support his family. If it is very well paid and also demanding he might wish to spend on it only the time he needs to earn enough to live on. But he is forced to work full-time because there is no provision for doing the job on a part-time basis. For another man or woman the important job might be unpaid voluntary work, to which most time and energy are devoted. But because it is unpaid, a full-time paid job has to be done as well, leaving no time for recreation, social life or personal interests.

A married woman working as a newspaper advertisement clerk spends two evenings a week running a youth club, the job that really interests her and for which she has a talent. She would like to devote more time to the youth club and the club could use more of her time. The work is paid, though not so well as the newspaper job, and she would gladly take the cut in income if she could work half time on the newspaper and half time on youth work. The newspaper does not employ people half time, so she keeps her full-time job for the income it brings, works at the youth club in the evenings because this is what she regards as her 'real' occupation, and finds that she has too little time for the recreations and personal interests she needs if she is to give her best in youth work.

Part-time working provides a solution for many of these difficulties and offers most people the possibility of organizing a much better balance of activities. Everybody who wanted to work would be able to do some but nobody would have to work longer hours than he wanted to or needed to in order to earn a living. Moreover, by combining contrasting jobs on a part-time basis and by working part time at lower-paid jobs with high interest content, more workers would be able to make the business of earning a living a time of much greater recreational and personal interest value than it is at the moment.

When a man works all the week at one job, then if the job is not one that particularly engages his interest he must try to fit all the other activities he needs into what time is left to him. If he spends the same amount of time on two jobs, a well-chosen combination may go at least some way towards providing the other activities he needs. The factory worker doing a forty-hour week or more may in that time have satisfied nothing more than the need for a living wage. If he spent half that time in a shop or driving a bus he would add other satisfactions without increasing his hours of work. He would have a change of some recreational value. He might find some social activity in his second job or he might be able to pursue a personal interest or achieve a measure of self-development. All these forms of satisfaction are those which he would otherwise only begin to look for after work, and they would all have to compete for his time and attention when he was already too weary to do much that required mental or physical effort.

The two-job man would probably try to take one job for the money and the other for its personal satisfaction. In doing so he would achieve many of the satisfactions associated with leisure while still gainfully employed. An element of recreation, some social life, the pursuit of a personal interest and some self-development could all, in varying degrees, come from the two-job combination. Many of the part-time jobs that would be available would be those which at present, because he cannot do his first job part time, he has to do for nothing in his spare time. Social work for youth or old people is an example of this.

After work, the two-job man is therefore much better placed to make the most of his leisure and to get real recreation, satisfaction and enjoyment from it. He finishes work fresher than the one-job man; change has left him less fatigued and he has taken care not to lumber himself with two physically exhausting part-time jobs. Being fresher, he has more time effectively available for leisure activity since he does not need time, or not so much time, to recover from exhaustion.

With more usable spare time, he has fewer activities to cram into it. Work and leisure have already merged to the extent that he has found some of the interests associated with leisure in the course of his varied working hours. What he will want to do after work is not to cram the whole of his personal life into a few

103

hours but to fill in the gaps left by his paid occupations.

As a one-job man Bill Smith used to work all day as a clerk and spend all his spare time on do-it-yourself jobs around the home. Carpentering, painting and decorating gave him a craft satisfaction that he could not get in an office, and most of his spare time went on it. His wife was glad to have the house so well cared for but the couple had no social life together. Bill could never be prized from the house for evenings out and yet his wife saw little of him at home: he always seemed to be hard at work in his garden shed or sleeping in front of the TV.

A two-job arrangement will make a big difference to Bill's leisure. He will cut back his clerk's job to half time and spend half his working week doing the challenging decorating jobs that give him so much satisfaction. At the end of the day he will have time to take his wife out occasionally. He may take part in social activities, do some reading or study a new skill which will add to his personal self-development.

Jean Hardy used to be a dedicated committee woman with little time for her husband and children. In addition to her full-time job as a secretary she was active in the Townswomen's Guild, the Community Welfare Society and the local school board, and was also a magistrate. She was out most evenings for meetings and fitted in her home and children between work and meetings. By keeping on the move sixteen hours a day and by highly efficient organization she was just able to keep abreast of her commitments. Her children had a programmed hour a day of her time, her husband was down in her diary for a once-a-month evening out, meals were prepared the previous evening and housework done at weekends and late at night. Neither husband nor children cared much for these arrangements and Mrs Hardy herself, when relaxing at home from her public charm, was frequently snappy with her nearest and dearest. Neighbours wondered how she did it all and predicted a crack-up.

Cutting her job in half with no loss of status or responsibility will make a big difference to Mrs Hardy's leisure. She will be less tired, have more time at home with the children, spend more time with her husband and still have time for a relaxing hobby. Eventually she may drop her over-extended committee work in favour of a part-time job running the local community welfare society. As soon as the children are off their hands Jean Hardy's husband will go on to half time at his engineering job and start to carry out his plan to build up into a profitable business his hobby of designing metal jewellery. In this

104

way he too will be able to spend more time at home.

Technology is rapidly transforming the age of overtime into the age of leisure. Without part-time working, the average working week is likely to shrink considerably in the next few years, the retirement age is likely to be reduced and holidays lengthened. Everyone in work can expect to have more leisure. Many workers in Britain and America view this prospect with fear. They have been conditioned to work hard and have had little or no education in how to use leisure without literally boring themselves to death. Having time on one's hands is by no means necessarily a recipe for increasing happiness. It could easily lead to intense depression and alienation from society, even if livelihood is not a problem.

Multipurpose Man is better equipped than others to turn this challenge into an opportunity. Fear of leisure derives mainly from lack of imagination and initiative. In many jobs neither of these qualities is required of a worker in a sense that involves a call on his personal resources. His time is largely ordered by the requirements of his job and once the job is mastered the only imagination and initiative required are encompassed by the ability to spot familiar elements in a new situation and apply familiar procedures to it.

The two-job man makes use of imagination and initiative on his own behalf, not just on behalf of his employer. If he is to create his own pattern of employment successfully he needs to be a self-starter. He must be able to see what sort of a person he wants to be and how he wants his life to be balanced. He must be able to make things happen to fit his own plans. He must be master of his fate in a way that the full-time employee rarely is.

Nobody will acquire initiative simply by changing from one full-time job to two part-time ones. Yet the change itself is an exercise of initiative. And in a society where such changes are made as a matter of course by most workers, the habit of personal initiative will be encouraged. To make the best use of a two-job system, the worker needs to be ready and able to change from one part-time job to another as frequently as opportunity and his own inclination suggest.

He will be used to thinking in terms of starting something new and making his own decisions about how his life is to be organized. These qualities will be useful in his working life and they will stand him in good stead when increasing spare time gives him leisure opportunities he never had before.

For the two-job man more leisure time means more opportunity. He is already used to a wider world than just one place of work and his local community, and this has given him a broader view of possible ways of spending his time. It has also got him into the habit of thinking of time as an asset into which a new activity can be fitted, not as a desert to be crossed.

With this habit of mind already applying to his work, the two-job man finds it easier to look at leisure in the same way. A leisure activity becomes another project to be planned, prepared for and embarked on. The same initiative that motivates a man to leave one job and start another which interests him more will motivate him to start other activities which interest him and which differ from his work only in that they are not paid. Leisure becomes a chance for him to do many of the things he has always wanted to do, without the tiresome necessity of finding someone prepared to pay him.

With this approach the two-job man never realizes that he has a leisure problem. There are always activities in which he wants to interest himself. When the paid activities take up less time, he can devote more to the unpaid ones. Long before today's forty-hour week has shrunk to tomorrow's thirty-hour week or twenty-five-hour week the two-job man will have got used to periods when he is working only part-time at paid work, spending some of his time studying or learning a new skill. The age of leisure will be a golden age to him when he can pursue more of his real interests.

More and more of these real interests will be active ones, by which is meant actively absorbing or collating information as well as performing physical actions. Since his new leisure will be based on habits of work, he will approach leisure in a positive way, putting something into it instead of passively waiting to get something out of it. He will still want to be entertained and amused, and will still want to relax. The difference will be that there will be less strain from which to relax. Nothing is so boring as a holiday when one has done nothing to take a holiday *from*, as many a rich playboy has discovered.

For the two-job man the new life of leisure will never be a holiday. He will probably employ less of it on being entertained, than he does now, and less of it in playing games for relaxation. He will continue to want to stretch himself and his abilities and will use his extra time to do this. He will want to serve the community in voluntary work, research a subject which interests him, try his hand at writing, composing, painting or the performing arts, practise a craft. His horizon will never be limited by beer and bingo; he will have things to do and will be happy doing them.

106

In doing things instead of being entertained he will solve one of the main difficulties about extra leisure, shortage of money. Being entertained costs money and the reason many people with extended leisure cannot fully enjoy it is that they have been conditioned to regard as time to be filled with entertainment, which usually has to be paid for. The popularity of fishing stems partly from the fact that this sport provides the maximum duration of entertainment, of a sort, for the minimum of financial outlay.

Ironically, it is in some cases an inability to fill leisure today which makes a man a moonlighter. Shift workers particularly, enjoying time off during the day when others are at work and feeling somewhat at a loss, take second jobs to fill in the empty hours. The habit of industry thus acquired might well help a man to make creative use of his new opportunities when shorter hours bring more leisure time for all.

Chapter ten

Could we make the change?

A two-job economy offers the citizen of an industrial society an opportunity to live a much fuller, more rewarding and more enjoyable working life than most of today's workers can expect. But is it a practical way to organize life in a nation which has for centuries been dedicated to the concept of one man, one job? And if it is practicable, would managements and trade unions stand for so radical a departure from positions which they have defended passionately over the years? Is the ordinary worker ready to change his life style in so thoroughgoing a way?

It is clear that multiple part-time working can only flourish if two basic conditions are met. One is that there is a high level of employment and that varied forms of employment are readily available. This condition is met in parts of Britain and America but is certainly not found in either country as a whole.

The second condition is that it is possible for a man to live at a basic level on a half-time pay packet, relying on the other half to provide the jam on the bread and butter. This is at present true only of a minority of jobs but their number is growing. As automation eliminates many of the more menial and unproductive jobs the proportion of better-paid ones must increase.

Yet if multiple part-time working requires a high level of varied employment, it is also true that the pressures of unemployment could give an impetus to new thinking about work-patterns. The growth of fuller employment after a period of high unemployment could provide just the climate of optimism, enterprise and prosperity which the introduction of new working arrangements requires. Economic stress generates a climate favourable to radical new thinking and a buoyant period after a recession would be a favourable time to put this new thinking into practice. Planning for the organized introduction of multiple part-time working could also play a part in alleviating some of the problems of unemployment.

To some extent unemployment pushes workers into part-time

working, though it does so under most unfavourable circumstances. When work is short and large-scale redundancies threaten, many workers prefer some form of work-sharing to widespread lay-offs. In industries most immediately threatened, factories may go on short time and workers who were once doing overtime in a regular forty-five or fifty-hour week find themselves working three days a week, perhaps twenty-four hours in all. Their pay will be very low because their previous high earnings depended on overtime rates to boost a poor basic rate. Working half time, they will get considerably less than half their full-time pay. This is sometimes made up by the wives working part time.

In industries not so immediately threatened there are demands for a reduction of working hours and for earlier retirement as a means of sharing out the available work. This coincides with a general demand for more leisure, particularly in stress jobs. There are demands in the USA for hours of work to be reduced to thirty without loss of earnings.

All this creates a situation in which, sometimes against their will, large numbers of workers previously employed full time find themselves working part time or on short time. This in turn may give rise to an urge to explore new fields of employment, if only temporarily. Factory workers on short time frequently seek to top up their earnings by window-cleaning, decorating, electrical repairs or other services. Their wives work in shops and offices. For some workers a sort of double-job work pattern emerges, though in the most disadvantageous of conditions.

At the same time, the threat of further redundancies in a dying or contracting industry creates a demand for the establishment of retraining facilities and for the setting up of new industries to create new jobs. If the recession continues and worsens, and trends seem to offer no prospect of a quick improvement, there will be a further demand for more radical measures. When the economy is seen not to be working, and the traditional ways of organizing society can be seen to have failed, then people are ready to listen to new ideas. In these circumstances, ideas which represent a sharp break with past practice are particularly welcome.

What usually happens is that when the economy picks up, whether as a result of government measures or simply in the normal cyclical fashion nobody seems quite to understand, work patterns return to 'normal'. If any industry is permanently contracting its labour force, as steel and mining have been doing, then workers drift away to work full time at new or revived industries. Where the industry is subject to quick turns of fortune, like the motor-car industry, short-time working rapidly gives way first to full-time, then to overtime working and the whole unbalanced business starts all over again.

It is at this point—during the recession and before the post-recession pick-up has got under way—that multiple part-time working can best be considered and planned for. Used intelligently as a friend instead of an enemy, Multipurpose Man could help to ensure that violent swings between overtime and short time are evened out, and contracting industries shed workers slowly enough for them to be easily reabsorbed elsewhere.

It is psychologically difficult to institute a radical change during a period of settled prosperity. It is easy to carry out experiments in such a period, however, if the decision to make changes has been taken earlier during a period of difficulty and urgency.

If the decision has been taken during a period of relatively high unemployment to encourage part-time working as a possible option, the time to put it into effect is when the economy starts to recover. It is at this moment that industries on short time normally restore the old working week and employees give up whatever outside jobs they have picked up and resume full-time work.

This is the time when workers could be told that while they could go back to the old hours if they wished, they could equally, if they preferred, stay on short time and keep whatever outside job they had. If they chose to stay part-timers they would be guaranteed the same security of tenure in the part-time job that they had in their full-time jobs. Pensions, holidays and other accumulated benefit rights would be retained as a proportion of their full-time rights.

If a firm's recovery took it from short time to a position in which it would normally go on to overtime, there would again be a different procedure. Regular, permanent overtime would be banned. Extra production would be achieved by taking on part-time workers and these would have the same status as full-time men, with benefits pro rata. A later run-down, if necessary, could be achieved by stopping recruiting and allowing for normal wastage. The part-timers would not be casuals. They would have assured, regular jobs earning proportionately all benefits and paid at the same scale. There being no regular overtime, the unions would negotiate for their men and women a new basic rate which would give a good wage for a normal week's work and the part-time worker would get his proportion of this.

If it ever became desirable to increase the proportion of part-timers, then by agreement between management and the unions, the part-timers could be offered a rate slightly higher than the exact proportion of the time worked.

After experience of the ups and downs of factory work or the insecurity inherent in a declining industry many workers might well prefer to hold on to any second job they had already acquired and take up the part-time option when the factory or works resumed full-time working. As the economy picked up, other jobs would become progressively easier to find and part-time working would gain more adherents. New industries and factories newly expanding might welcome the flexibility offered by the availability of part-time labour.

Even in good times there are places where one job is hard enough to find, let alone two. This will be eased to some extent as communications improve and it becomes easy to work in a town thirty or forty miles away. Multiple part-time working will itself also help to create new jobs, since many previously unpaid voluntary jobs will become paid part-time jobs and there will be a growth in the variety of service jobs available on a part-time basis.

The problem of variety in jobs is one that will have to be solved whether or not Multipurpose Man comes on the scene. The experience of whole areas depending on one industry and dying when that industry declines has shown that the one-industry town is a dangerous anachronism today. A varied spread of employment must be provided in every region. When it is, men who remember the one-industry days will appreciate that a one-industry man in a period of economic transition can be as vulnerable to personal disaster as a worker in a one-industry town.

A system of part-time double-jobbing would cause a number of administrative difficulties. In a society planned for workers doing one job each, the widespread introduction of double-jobbing would give rise to many difficulties in calculating tax payments, benefits and entitlements arising from employment. National insurance contributions, sickness benefits, unemployment pay, holiday entitlement, superannuation and pensions of all kinds, season tickets and income tax are all calculated on the basis of a worker getting all his earned income from one full-time source.

Double-jobbing would also complicate the administration of means-tested social service benefits and rebates. The benefits and rebates themselves would not have to be changed but the establishment of means on which they are based would become more difficult.

Nor is this a problem simply for the very lowest paid. In Britain means-tested benefits can in some circumstances affect many members of the middle class, for instance when a family applies for assistance with boarding school fees or university education.

None of these admitted difficulties makes double-jobbing impossible, since some millions of the population are already doing more than one job in one form or another. No doubt today's moonlighters include some who are not over-scrupulous about declaring all their earnings and a certain amount of tax dodging takes place. If double-jobbing were widely extended without reforming the tax system the loss to the Inland Revenue might be considerable.

Even the present level of part-time working has shown the need for administrative changes in many of the worker's dealings with the state and public authorities. A national part-time work commission could be set up to examine existing administration as it affects the part-time worker and suggest amendments which would relate his responsibilities and benefits to the hours he works at his job. Clearly the system would have to be made sensitive to frequent changes of hours worked and income earned. At the same time it would have to be simplified to deal with perhaps double the present number of individual work situations. The growing use of computers to deal with administrative routine of this sort should ensure that this is not an insoluble problem.

The commission's brief would be to ensure that for both the employer and the worker part-time work would be no more expensive in administration and incidental costs than full-time work. Where necessary, the commision would have to instruct public bodies to make arrangements to accommodate part-timers. Season tickets, for instance, are issued only on the basis of a worker making the same double journey five days a week. The basis might have to be changed to a saving based on regular use of public transport in any direction. Ultimately, free city transport might be the answer.

All pensions would have to be fully transferable and available to part-timers on a proportionate basis. It might be necessary to phase out individual firms' pension schemes in favour of central schemes into which both employers and employees would pay contributions. Employers could pay in on the basis of their employees' earnings and workers would pay a fixed percentage of their earnings from any source. The practice of tying a man to a job by means of accumulated non-transferable pension rights would have to end.

Many of the fringe benefits employers at present offer would be

112

provided on a regional basis rather than by individual companies. Instead of one firm providing a sports field exclusively for its own employees, all the employers in an area could contribute according to the size of their payroll to the provision of sports facilities for all workers and their families in the locality.

Many firms which regard themselves as good employers are already hostile to part-time working on the grounds that part-timers cannot give the firm the complete loyalty to which the firm feels entitled as some return for the benefits it provides. On the other hand, 'loyalty' as a duty over and above the requirement to do a conscientious day's work is already being increasingly repudiated by today's full-time workers. In business, workers are now demanding a strictly businesslike relationship based on an equitable contract with no special favours. Part-time working would simply accelerate a move towards a worker-management relationship of mutual respect and independence. It represents a further stage in the process by which the old-time boss becomes the new-style team leader.

Although some of the administrative changes might be complicated, the existence of large numbers of part-timers today shows that none of them are impossible. All that is required to make the necessary changes is the will to put the part-timer on a fair and equitable basis in relation to the full-timer. Much more difficult than the administrative mechanics of making the change to multiple part-time working will be necessary new thinking. Changing the minds and entrenched attitudes of employers and workers and their respective organizations will not be as easy as changing the pensions rules or insurance arrangements.

Employers are often suspicious of part-timers even in the low-status casual jobs to which they are usually relegated today. The part-timer cannot be fully dedicated to the company's interests or he would not be content to work part time. Employers have reckoned that the pay-packet should buy a worker's full involvement in the business, so that he stands ready to do whatever extra work is required of him beyond his nominal working hours. Local government workers, for instance, subscribe to a code of conduct under which they are bound to give their undivided loyalty to their employers. Even among full-time workers, however, such concepts are losing their force. Cases have come to light of town clerks doing legal business on the side, and many lower-grade local government workers have spare-time jobs, though these are frowned upon by their superiors.

There is a widespread employers' prejudice against part-timers on the grounds that they are not serious workers, being only interested in making a little money with the least possible effort. In so far as there is any truth in this, the employers themselves are largely to blame, since in many cases it is only the casual, unskilled jobs which are open to part-timers. Opening up to part-timers more responsible jobs, including executive and supervisory grades, will require a massive operation to overcome encrusted prejudice among employers. Splitting executive jobs in two is designed to eradicate just that obsessive over-dedication and overwork, often leading to a health breakdown, which old-style employers have looked for as evidence that the executive is pulling his weight. It is going to be hard to persuade them that the cool, unharassed executive who appears two days a week can be a better salary investment.

Fears that part-time work above the casual unskilled level would be hard to schedule and would disrupt the running of a firm are answered by the experiences of firms which have gone over to a four-day week. This is not part-time working, since the four days are lengthened to give a forty-hour week. But it can involve the firm shutting down on Fridays when customers will be at work and it was felt that the absence of anyone to take orders or answer queries could lose the firm business. In practice this has not happened. Customers have quickly adjusted to the fact that the firm is not open on Fridays, just as customers have previously adjusted to firms not being open on Saturday mornings. What matters is how efficient the service is when the firm *is* at work. Even when firms work conventional hours particular executives are frequently unavailable for days at a time when away on business trips. Either someone else handles the query or it is left a few days until the man gets back to his desk.

Fears of part-time working among trade unionists are quite as strong as those of employers. Like those of the employers, the union men's fears are based on traditional habits of thought. There is first of all the fear of divided loyalty. Until now unions have depended for their strength on the unity and loyalty of their members. That unity and that loyalty have depended on the trust and fellowship which grow when men work side by side at the same job. Miners, who often live in self-contained groups as well as working together, have formed particularly strong bonds of mutual loyalty and their union strength is formidable as a result. Would this powerful community spirit survive at full strength if they worked only part time in the mines and spent half the week doing something else? As one union

114

man said, 'If all our people were working part time, we'd have to organize twice as many of them in a strike to get the same result.' If a man worked at two jobs, he might have to join two unions, with consequent divided loyalties.

Equally deep-rooted is the suspicion of any training or retraining which seems to short-cut the traditional apprenticeship or qualifying period. Craft unions were deeply suspicious of dilutees—quickly-trained men and women—whom they had to accept during the war. Teachers were equally suspicious of those trained in emergency two-year courses after the war. They pressed successfully for the three-year training course to be resumed as soon as possible. In these and other cases it was feared that any dilution of training procedures would lower the status of the job and also lower the workers' bargaining power.

Unions have also had a further fear that part-timers will be used by employers to undercut or displace full-time employees. They have been able to reassure themselves about undercutting by insisting that part-timers must be paid the same hourly rate as full-timers. But the fear remains that if the full-timers were not there in strength to protect both the part-timers and themselves, the part-timers would be vulnerable to attacks on their living standards. Unless rigorously controlled from the start, the weaker part-time brothers would be used to displace full-time men, and once this had been done their wages would be cut.

These are powerful and very real fears, based on bitter past experience, but they are not necessarily valid for the future. Conditions which gave rise to them are passing, even without the introduction of multiple part-time working. The acceptance of part-time working, and planning for it, could remove the grounds for such misgivings.

The old close, tribal solidarity of self-contained working groups, though still strong today, is already passing without any help from part-timers. Both the docks and the mines, where such clan feeling has been strongest, are in some respects declining industries; the old communities are being broken up. Traditional solidarity may well survive and flourish but it can no longer be based on the old exclusivism which made dockers and miners members of self-contained communities largely out of contact with the rest of the world.

Union solidarity can still be a powerful weapon in the economic struggle. It is based today more on hard-headed economic logic than on traditional emotion, but it is none the less effective for that. Part-timers, as one union man foresaw, can actually increase union

115

strength if they can be organized. If a man has another part-time job, and his wife has one too, he cannot easily be starved into submission. While the insistence on full apprenticeships is as strong as ever in the craft unions, and rightly, there is already new thinking about retraining which owes nothing to part-timers, though part-timers could benefit from it. Both employers and unions have seen benefits in greater job flexibility within an industry, and a skilled craftsman in the engineering industry can train within the industry for another skill which will increase his employment opportunities and break down the rigid distinctions between one skilled operation and another.

While the need for full training in the first place is insisted on more strongly than ever, it is recognized that some part of the training content of a skilled apprenticeship is valid over a whole range of different skills. In training a skilled worker for a new skilled job in the same industry, it is not necessary to go again over this common ground. The training of a skilled worker for a new skilled job can therefore be substantially reduced in time without reducing training standards.

Both employers and unions have recognized that a man with more than one skill, able to do a wider range of jobs, is more useful, and should be paid more, than a one-skill man. Although such job flexibility is at present confined to members of one union within one industry the advantages such flexibility brings could cut across the traditional union and industrial boundaries. Even if these barriers prove difficult to cross, the scope for job flexibility will be widened as unions amalgamate into ever larger and more comprehensive bodies.

The fear of part-timers being at the mercy of employers, unless a strong body of full-timers is there to protect the interests of all workers, could also be made obsolete by events. When part-timers are pin-money amateurs the fear is a real one: in the past whole industries have suffered low wage rates because most of the labour was supplied by wives or daughters who were in effect subsidized by their husbands or parents. The new part-timers would be a quite different breed, independent and determined to get full value for their work. Led by modernized trade unions attuned to their needs and able to organize them effectively, they could prove equally militant and even more successful than their full-time predecessors in gaining economic advances.

The danger is that both employers and unions may oppose a change of work pattern simply out of fear that the new pattern would put them at a disadvantage under present conditions. In doing so they would be ignoring the fact that different work patterns would create new conditions. Under new conditions, advantages for both management and labour would be greater if the new pattern were to be welcomed and planned for instead of just happening in a haphazard way. Just as there is a need for a national commission to plan the legislative and administrative changes that would be necessary, so there should also be a joint management-union body to think about the implications together and plan the new areas of agreement that would be needed to make the new pattern work smoothly for the benefit of all concerned.

To make the change to a new work pattern will require the sort of bold, radical new thinking we have learned not to expect from employers, unions or governments of any political complexion. Nor is there any reason to suppose that massive popular demand for change will stimulate new thought. If the present system were working reasonably well, and if it were seen to be likely to go on working reasonably well, the chances of carrying through the changes here envisaged would be slim indeed.

But the present system is not working well. In many jobs the workers are bored out of their minds. Many other jobs are likely to disappear through rationalization in the next few years. And many jobs have already disappeared for ever, creating for the first time since the war a large body of permanent unemployed. From these deep-seated ills have sprung waves of strikes and industrial unrest which have shaken the British economy to its foundations. Similar economic troubles will increase in other advanced countries for the same reasons.

As industrial troubles mount, bodies not usually given to radical thinking may be prepared to look sympathetically on any plan that might help to alleviate the situation. When other, more orthodox palliatives have failed to solve the problem of the seventies, Multipurpose Man may be thought worth trying.

The advent of the new versatile part-timer may be eased by the fact that he is not a revolutionary. No instant overthrow of established practices is required. No coercion of any kind is involved. Nobody will be forced to change his way of life. Some legislative and administrative changes will be needed but these will be permissive only. They will enlarge the options available to the individual; but they will not force him to abandon any present practice that seems good to him. The dedicated one-job man devoting his whole life to a single field of

117

work will be able to carry on exactly as before if that is what he wants. The difference will be that he will no longer be forced to stay all his life in a job which frustrates, or bores, or exhausts him. Some new thinking is required, but no immediate new investment. Some extra tolerance, but no dangerous, new, irreversible change of course.

Perhaps Multipurpose Man's greatest asset in winning a place in public life, indeed, is his unaggressive good manners. He treads on no political toes. He does not demand a stand-up fight to establish himself or a wholesale violent smashing of existing practice. He does not even require a fanfare of trumpets. He can come in modestly, quietly, to get on with his several jobs, leaving his virtues to speak for themselves.

All that is needed in the first instance is that the door shall be opened to him. There is no particular need for a factory to make a dramatic decision about the merits of full-or part-time work and opt for one or the other. Many people will want to go on doing one job all the time and there is no reason why they should not continue to do so happily. They are more likely to do so contentedly if they know that they could, if they wanted to, spend half the week doing something else.

The only decision needed is the permissive one that a prospective employee need not choose between total commitment and nothing. Part-time working does not have to be imposed by decree. It merely needs to be acknowledged as an acceptable option. The speed at which it catches on will obviously depend on the local availability of alternative employments and the satisfactions it is seen to offer as a way of life.

It is not necessary to wait for conditions favouring multiple part-time working to be established everywhere before giving it a try. It can grow up as conditions become favourable in a particular locality and as workers discover and try out the possibilities for themselves. It is not an irrevocable pattern. A man who changes jobs, or takes on two part-time jobs, does not commit himself for life to double-jobbing. He can at any time go back to concentrate on one job if he finds that it suits him better to do so. People can do it if they wish, stop doing it if they wish, or ignore the whole idea if they wish. It is an extra option, not a straitjacket.

Multiple part-time working will bring economic advantage to the country by providing a much more flexible labour force in a time of transition. It will provide a safety-valve and a protection against industrial unrest, at a time when a shrinking labour market threatens immense social upheaval. But it is not just an economic device. It is primarily an adventure of the imagination proposed for the enrichment of working life, and so of life as a whole. It is proposed as a means of widening the worker's outlook and setting him free from an age-old bondage.

As the industrial nations of the world move through the technological revolution into the era of automation and personal aspiration, the lifetime drudge of factory, mine or office will be seen to be the obsolete figure he is. Multipurpose Man, questing, fresh-minded and many-sided, livelier, happier and more fulfilled, will be the new man for the new age.

Footnotes

CHAPTER ONE

1 'Blue Collar Blues on the Assembly Line': Judson Gooding, *Fortune*, July 1970.

2 Interview with the author, 23 September 1970.
3 *The Times*, 20 November 1970.
4 *The Times*, 25 August 1970.

5 'Fight Facing British Cars': Paddy McGarvey, *Sunday Telegraph*, 9 August 1970.

6 'Frustration as a Cause of Inflation': John Nelson, *The Times*, 15 February 1971.

7 'It Pays to Wake Up the Blue Collar Worker': Judson Gooding, *Fortune*, September 1970.

CHAPTER TWO

1 'The Second-Job Mystery': John Yates, *New Society*, 25 May 1972.

2 'Moonlighting: An Economic Phenomenon': H.R. Hamel and F.A. Bogan, *Monthly Labour Review* (USA) No. 90, October 1967.

3 'Multiple Jobholders in 1964': Hamel and Bogan, *Monthly Labour Review* (USA) No. 88, March 1965.

CHAPTER FOUR

1 'When There's More to Life than Work': Ian Brown, *Daily Mail*, 18 March 1971

CHAPTER SIX

1 George Teeling-Smith, Director of the Office of Health Economics, Royal Society of Health Congress, Eastbourne, 1972.

2 Speech to Institute of Personnel Management, 1972.

DATE DUE